All poems written by Baxter Black
Copyright © 2000 by Baxter Black

Published by: **Coyote Cowboy Company**
P.O. Box 2190
Benson, Arizona 85602
All rights reserved

Cover design by Jay Dusard
LIBRARY OF CONGRESS CATALOGING IN PUBLICATION DATA
Main entry under:
Cowboy Poetry
Bibliography: p
1. Coyote Cowboy Poetry
2. Cowboy-Poetry
3. Poetry-Cowboy
4. Humor-Cowboy
5. Agriculture-Poetic Comment

I. Black, Baxter Ashby, 1945-

Library of Congress #00-091189
ISBN 0-939343-30-4

OTHER BOOKS BY BAXTER

* THE COWBOY AND HIS DOG © 1980
* A RIDER, A ROPER AND A HECK'UVA WINDMILL MAN © 1982
ON THE EDGE OF COMMON SENSE, THE BEST SO FAR © 1983
* DOC, WHILE YER HERE © 1984
BUCKAROO HISTORY © 1985
COYOTE COWBOY POETRY © 1986
✔ CROUTONS ON A COW PIE © 1988
✔ THE BUCKSKIN MARE © 1989
✔ COWBOY STANDARD TIME © 1990
CROUTONS ON A COW PIE, VOL 2 © 1992
HEY, COWBOY, WANNA GET LUCKY? © 1994 *(Crown Publishing, Inc.)*
✗ DUNNY AND THE DUCK © 1994
✗ COW ATTACK © 1996
CACTUS TRACKS AND COWBOY PHILOSOPHY © 1997
(Crown Publishing, Inc.)
✗ LOOSE COW PARTY © 1998

* included in Coyote Cowboy Poetry 1986
✔ included in Croutons On A Cow Pie, Vol 2 1992
✗ included in A Cowful of Cowboy Poetry 2000

FORWARD

I was at a bull sale when an old friend came up to me and said, "Your last article was the best thing I ever read." Naturally, the comment enlarged my stature in my eyes and gave me a 'writer's high'.

At the time I paid little attention to the fact that I had never written for the publication where my friend said the article appeared. He could have been mixed-up, disoriented. But it was I who would come crashing to the ground later when my friend reappeared and said, "I must apologize. I was confused. You didn't write that article. Baxter Black did. I bet you wish you had written it, huh?"

Of course I did. What a silly question. I don't know of a single cowboy columnist, farm broadcaster, cowboy poet or traveling troubadour who doesn't wish they had what Baxter has. Whatever "it" is. I haven't a clue. I do remember when I witnessed Baxter's special gift for the first time. He was performing in front of a large convention crowd wearing a gaudy purple wild rag around his neck, a well worn cowboy hat worn well, and an American flag for a shirt. But that wasn't why the convention goers saluted him with a standing ovation.

If I had to guess, I'd say Baxter's secret is that he is one of us… only a whole lot more so. A roper, a horseshoer and a heck of a gate opener for sure. I know that for a fact. Two hours after I shook his hand for the first time Baxter was entertaining my cows and I from a podium atop a stack of hay in the back of my truck. Even the cows thought Baxter was something special, although I think that was because he was parceling out way more hay per cow than I usually do.

Because I think Baxter's brain is unique I pick it every chance I get. I remember a long time ago asking him why he didn't "Go for the big time, take his act to Hollywood, his novel to New York and his poetry to Carnegie Hall." Baxter replied that, no, he knew his audience and wasn't going to change who he was. He would not forsake his world to enter theirs. He didn't have to. It turns out the rest of the English speaking world loves Baxter as much as we country folks do. These days when Baxter takes his show on the road he's just as apt to end up on a stage in Las Vegas, Nevada, as he is one in Las Vegas, New Mexico. Only Baxter could make both crowds howl with laughter, jump to their feet and clap till their hands hurt.

To say that Baxter is a cowboy poet is like saying that the Southwest he adores is just a desert; the Grand Canyon a big hole in the ground. I could use up the words in three dictionaries and still not convey the essence of the man. There's not a communication medium he hasn't conquered: television, radio, print, even the Internet. He's a brilliant novelist, columnist, cartoonist, musician and entertainer. He writes so well he can make you cry from sadness or from laughing too hard.

I used to wonder why someone who trained so long and hard to become a distinguished veterinarian would give it all up for a chance to speak at a Farm Bureau meeting. After becoming his friend I realized that Baxter could no more stop himself from being a great entertainer than a cow can keep from being a bovine.

While I may not know HOW Baxter does it, I think I know WHY. Because he loves farmers and ranchers and the simple lives we lead. And we in turn love him. We consider him family because Baxter has taken our way of life, and in some small way, ourselves, into the living rooms, banquet halls and bookstores of America. He has been kind enough to take us all along for the ride. And boy, has it been fun! In doing so Baxter has made us all feel just a little bit better about ourselves. About who we are.

Come to think of it, that may be his secret after all. You can't spend any time at all with Baxter and not feel a little better for having done so. As anyone who reads this book will attest.

Lee Pitts
Commission man, editor of the Livestock Market Digest and in Baxter's words, the best agricultural writer in America.

TABLE OF CONTENTS

A COWFUL

Grandpa Tommy's dad used to say "A cowful is a great sufficiency." According to my research, the rumen on a mature cow can hold over 300 pounds. And by anybody's standards that is a substantial quantity.

Say you had a cowful of pocket change. You'd almost need a cow to keep it in. Say you had a cowful of wet laundry. It would take a forklift to get it in the dryer. Say you had a cowful of manure. Well, I guess a lot of us do.

If cowful became an accepted unit of measure it could replace the antiquated English standards like the dram and the rod. And those bland, simple minded metric names that somehow sound communistic; kiloliter, hectometer, decigram. Can you picture in your mind a decigram? Is it the weight of a decimated graham cracker? Or ten grandmas standin' on the scale?

Under the cowful system 15 scoopfuls would equal a cowful. Two bootfuls would make a scoopful, two hatfuls would make a bootful. Half a hatful would equal a capful.

6 canfuls, as in beer cans, makes a capful. One canful equals 40 thimblefuls, 20 teardrops in a thimbleful.

The dosage for penicillin would read: 4 teardrops per 5 scoopfuls of body weight IM.

For Blackleg four-way vaccination: 1 thimbleful SQ. Repeat in 60 days.

Bizarre, you say. If cowful was a measure of weight or volume, possibly the distance between postholes would become the standard unit of measure for length, i.e. 660 post holes per section line - 4 thumbs to a hand, 3 hands to a foot, 4 feet to a coyote length and 2 coyote lengths to a posthole.

Decibels of loudness would be described in more understandable terms. From chicken peck to pig squeal for everyday sounds. Loud noises would be categorized as small wreck, big wreck and heck'uva wreck.

"So, did you hear about Orb gettin' bucked off? Musta sailed 5 coyote lengths, hit the side of the grain bin with a moose bugle and two cowfuls of pellets fell on him. Smashed him flatter'n a rabbit ear.

"They got him to the Doc in half a coon's age, transfused him with a six pack of type 0 negative and removed a posthole of intestine. He's doin' okay but he's lost about six hatfuls.

"He's been a sheep's gestation recovering. Doc says it's shock, but I figger it just scared a pea waddin' and a half out of him. Well, I gotta go. I've got an appointment in 4 1/2 shakes of a lamb's tail."

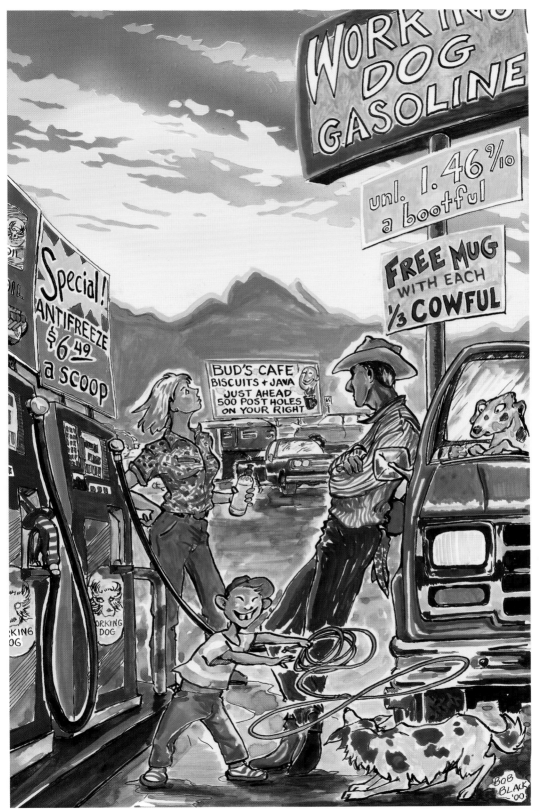

9

BARNYARD BESTSELLERS

From Barns & Stable Bestseller List.   Livestock are heavily into self-help books.

- <u>Herefords are from Venus - Angus are from Mars</u>
An example of prehistoric rivalry

- <u>Chicken Soup for Freshly Weaned Ruminant's Soul</u>
Heart wrenching stories of leaving home

- <u>The Holstein Prophecy</u>
Bovine angels inspire milkers to greater production

- <u>The Joy of Artificial Insemination</u>
Do the best you can with what you've got

- <u>The 7 Habits of Highly Effective Porcines</u>
How to organize your own pig pen

- <u>Co-Dependent No More: Breaking the Herd Habit</u>
Earn millions without leaving your stall

- <u>The 9 Steps to Parasitic Freedom</u>
Say good-bye to lice

- <u>The Goat That Listens To Horses</u>
Memoirs of a race track psychologist

- <u>One Day My Sole Just Opened Up</u>
The tale of one cow's battle with footrot

- <u>Protein Power</u>
Eat urea and like it

- <u>Don't Sweat the Small Stuff</u>
Shetlands improve their self-esteem

- <u>Cook Right for Your Type</u>
Rumen vs Stomach vs Gizzard

- <u>Into Thin Air</u>
Where your methane and money go

And lest you think ungulates don't read for fun, I offer these last titles.

<u>The Sheep Whisperer</u>
<u>The Cow From Snowy River</u>
<u>A Power Line Runs Through It</u>
<u>Feedlots of Madison County</u>
<u>The Dairy of Ann Frank</u>

IF THIS OL' HAT COULD TALK

"Ah, if this ol' hat could talk, it could tell a million stories..." What pictures we conjure up thinkin' about an old cowboy's hat. Shading his eyes from the sun, dippin' water out of a creek, fannin' a bronc. It sure captures the romantic image of our Great American Hero.

I'm not certain why the hat is the choice of fashion conscious folklorists focused on flattering the fedoraly friendly. But it is.

I mean, have you ever heard anyone say, "If these ol' socks could talk..." What would an old sock say?

"Ya know I've laid for days between his gnarled foot and the sole of his stinking boot. It's like being stuck to the bottom of a dumpster. When the duct tape wore thin, everything he walked in squished it's way inside. Dirt, cow manure, dust, cow manure, mud, cow manure.. well, you get the picture. And on those rare occasions when I saw daylight I was dryin' over a woodstove or airin' my holiness to the four strong winds hangin' on a bob wire fence. It is no life for the fastidious."

Or maybe... "If this ol' pocketknife could talk..."

"I've been with Jim Bob since he lost his yella Barlow in the chemical toilet at the ranch rodeo six years ago. If I'd a'known how bad I was gonna be treated, I'd a jumped in the bluewater, too. He don't seem to know the first thing about sharpenin' my blade. I've seen paper plates with a better edge. My tip's broke off from the time he tried to take the hubcap off his '69 Ford. One time he got mad and tried to stab a baked potato. Mashed it but never broke the skin..."

Or, "If this ol' moustache could talk..."

"I feel like a rest home for migrating lice. A birdhouse for nesting gnats. A picnic table for the common housefly. I get gnawed on, fondled, tugged, and twirled so much I feel like an easy date."

Or, "If this ol' pocket comb could talk..."

"If I lose one more tooth I'm gonna have to get an upper plate..."

Or, "If this ol' shirt pocket could talk..."

"The next time he puts a half chewed cud of Redman in me while he's havin' lunch, I'm gonna prolapse in his bowl of chili..."

Or, "If this ol' plastic sleeve could talk..."

Whoa, I'm beginning to see why those students of cowboy lore stick with the talking hat. It's hard to conjure up romantic images with a talking hearing aid or a reminiscing corn pad. But even with an ol' sombrero one takes a chance. I can remember getting sick in the back seat of my friend's new car. I found myself walking that fine line between good taste and throwing up in my hat. It was not an easy decision.

COW ATTACK

"What happened to your pickup seat? Is that buffalo track?"
Well, I guess you had to be there. We had a cow attack.
It all began when me and Roy went out to check the cows.
We'd finished lunch and watched our 'soap' and forced ourselves to rouse.

We's pokin' through the heavy bunch for calves to tag and check.
I spotted one but his ol' mom was bowin' up her neck.
She pawed the ground and swung her head a'slingin' froth and spit
Then bellered like a wounded bull. "Say, Roy," I said, "let's quit!"

But Roy was bent on taggin' him and thought to make a grab,
"Just drive up there beside the calf, I'll pull him in the cab."
Oh, great. Another stroke of genius, of cowboy derring do.
Shornuf when Roy nabbed the calf, his mama came in, too.

And I do mean climbed up in there! Got a foot behind the seat,
Punched a horn right through the windshield and she wasn't very neat.
She was blowin' stuff out both ends till the cab was slick and green.
It was on the floor and on the roof and on the calf vaccine.

If you've been inside a dryer at the local laundromat
With a bear and fifty horseshoes then you know just where I's at.
At one point she was sittin' up, just goin' for a ride
But then she tore the gun rack down, the calf jumped out my side.

I was fightin' with my door lock which she'd smashed a'passin' by
When she peeked up through the steering wheel and looked me in the eye.
We escaped like paratroopers out the window, landed clear.
But the cow just kept on drivin' cause the truck was still in gear.

She topped a hump and disappeared. The blinker light came on
But if she turned I just can't say, by then the truck was gone.
I looked at Roy, "My truck's a wreck. My coveralls are soaked.
I'll probably never hear again. I think my ankle's broke.

And look at you. Yer pitiful, all crumpled up and stiff.
Like you been eat by wild dogs and pooped over a cliff."
"But think about it," Roy said. "Since Grandpa was alive,
I b'lieve that that's the firstest time I've seen a cattle drive."

THE ROMANTIC COWBOY

There's nothing like an evening of calving to promote the romantic image of the cowboy. Right, ladies?

Don invited a nice woman out to his ranch one evening for candlelight, wine and canned bean dip. This dinner date coincided with calving season. After an hour of civilized conversation about French paintings, the European Common Market and the condition of the rodeo arena in Ponoka, Don invited his date to go with him to check the cows.

She didn't exactly squeal with delight but he explained how scientific livestock raising had become. "Almost like visiting a human hospital maternity ward," he said, authoritatively.

They drove his Bronco out into the calving pasture and immediately spotted a braymer cross cow tryin' to calve. "We'll watch her for a few minutes to see if everything comes out okay," suggested Don sliding an arm around her shoulders.

They sat in the warm cab, moonlight mixing with Don's elaborate discourse of bovine parturition. After half an hour he decided to assist the cow. Partly for the cow and partly to show off.

The calf appeared to be hiplocked.

His date prepared to see modern veterinary procedure save the day. Don drove up to the head end of the cow and left the headlights shining in her eyes. Sneaking out, he slipped around behind her. He slid the nylon obstetrical straps over the calf's protruding front feet. At first tug the cow arose like a bee stung buffalo!

She whirled to mash Don. He was jerked off his feet but clung to the straps as the cow chased him like a dog chasin' its tail! He was alternately upright, flat out, levitating, scooting, skiing, sliding, screaming and squirreling as the three of them circled like a shaky ceiling fan.

His only hope of survival was to hang on and stay behind the helicoptering cow. Even then she managed to land enough blows to win the round and tromp his fallen hat to a pulp.

On one mighty jerk, the calf popped out. Don executed a complete cartwheel and landed on his back. The cow rolled him once and headed off in the darkness.

His date, who had watched Don's calving technique from the cab was not impressed. "Less than professional," she had commented as he climbed in the cab after giving the departed cow a four alarm cussing.

Don tried to regain his composure and recapture the mood by explaining that he had been in control the whole time. However, it was not very convincing what with the big glob of manure plastered on the side of his neck and the piece of placenta dangling from his ear.

RICH FARMING

If wheat gets up to seven bucks I'll hoard it, yessiree
Till the grain bin's overflowin' or it gets back down to three.

There's too much ridin' on it to sell it right away,
The banker might call in my note, they're funny that-a-way.

As long as things are nip and tuck they'll let the balance ride.
Just pay the interest on it and they'll be satisfied.

They don't like sudden changes conservatives, you see,
They like things that they can count on like hail and CRP.

And if you look too prosperous or friends think that you are
They'll try and sell you somethin' you've lived without, so far,

Like asphalt on the driveway or fancy silverware
Or a double jointed tractor 'course, the preacher gets his share.

No, there ain't no use me gettin' rich, knowin' me, I'd spend it.
And borrow more for land and stock. There's plenty who would lend it.

I'm better off just gettin' by and stayin' where I set
'Cause the more that I make farmin' the more I go in debt.

So, if wheat gets up to seven I could sell it on the board
But I won't. 'Cause makin' money's one thing I can't afford.

It's a different kind of logic that allows a man to boast
When the richest farmer farmin' is the one who owes the most.

I KNOW YOU'LL MISS THIS MAN

The Lord spoke to the heavy hearts that stood with hats in hand

"Your sadness pains me deeply and I know you'll miss this man
But, it's true what you've been hearing, Heaven is a real place.
That's no small consolation. You should use that fact to face

The emptiness his parting left that seeps into your bones
And draw on it to ease your pain. For he is not alone.
You see, all his friends are up here and all his loved ones, too,
'Cause it wouldn't be a heaven without each one of you.

And heaven for a cowboy is just what you might expect,
It's horses that need tunin' up and heifers that need checked.
It's long rides with a purpose and a code that lights the way
And a satisfying reason to get up every day.

It's the ranch he's always dreamed of and never knew he'd find
And if you think about it, you can see it in your mind.
Him, leanin' in the saddle with his ol' hat on his head,
Contentment set upon his face like blankets on a bed.

The leather creaks a little as he shifts there in the seat.
The bit chains give a jingle when his pony switches feet.
And you somehow get the feelin' that he's sittin' on a throne
A'gazin' out on paradise just like it was his own.

I can promise you he's happy, though I know you can't pretend
You're glad he made the journey. It's too hard to comprehend.
The earthly way you look at things can never satisfy
Your lack of understanding for the answer to the 'Why?'

So, I offer this small comfort to put your grief to rest,
I only take the top hands 'cause my crew's the very best.
And I know it might seem selfish to friends and next of kin
But I needed one more cowboy and Billy fit right in."

THE WEST

They don't call it Death Valley for nuthin'
      And coyotes don't make a good pet
    But livin' out here with the griz and the deer
        you pretty much take what you get

And the Rockies have shoulders like granite
      They're big and they make their own rules
    So take what you need but you better pay heed
        'Cause the mountain don't tolerate fools

And the wind is the moan of the prairie
      That haunts and bedevils the plains
    The soul stealin' kind that can fray a man's mind
        Till only his whimper remains

You can stand in the canyon's cathedral
      Where water and sky never rest
    And know in your bones that the meek, on their own
        Will never inherit the West

It's wild and it's wide and it's lonesome
      Where the dream of first blood still survives
    And it beckons to those who can bid adios
        To the comfort of 8 to 5 lives

So come all you brave caballeros
      Cinch up and reach down inside
    Till you feel the heat, then take a deep seat
        'Cause the West, boys, she ain't broke to ride

ILLINOIS COWBOY

"Where were you born?" The reporter asked one of my Colorado cowboy friends.

"Iowa," he answered.

"Iowa!" she said. "Why did you move?"

"Because it's hard to be a cowboy in Iowa."

Well, it might be harder to be a cowboy in the Midwest but they've got a bunch of good ones anyway. No matter how much dependence modern cowmen place on man-made mechanical devices, there are times when nothin' beats a good roper a'horseback.

Illinois is an anthill of bovine activity. They have an abundance of cow calf operations and the state has ranked in the top ten in numbers of cattle on feed. So a "loose cow" is not an unusual occurrence. That's when a good cowboy comes in handy.

Dr. Matt has his veterinary clinic in one of the many small towns that dot the northwestern Illinois countryside. One afternoon he was processing a truckload of feeder steers in the back of his clinic.

Despite good help and good facilities, accidents can happen. A gate was left open and shornuf, one of the steers escaped. And, according to Rule #1 in the Guidebook of Loose Cattle, the steer headed straight for the center of town.

Matt leaped to his Toyota Batmobile and took up the chase as the girls in the office cheered him on and wished, not for the first time, they'd had a video camera.

The steer had the advantage. He was able to cut through lawns, across lots filled with farm implements, behind gas pumps and down sidewalks. He jaywalked with impunity.

He galloped into the bank drive-through, raised his tail to the pie-eyed teller and proceeded to circle the bank building. Matt careened into the drive-through hot on the trail. By using the parking lot and surrounding sidewalks, he was able to keep the steer circling the bank through the manicured lawn and decorative shrubbery.

Matt's radio crackled, "Chet's just pulled into the clinic, could you use some help?"

The steer broke for the high school. "Send him on," Matt yelled, "we're headed for the football field!"

The steer had slowed to a trot by the time Chet wheeled his pickup and trailer into the school parking lot. He unloaded his horse, grabbed his rope and mounted.

Matt said it was beautiful to watch. When Chet rode through the goal posts the steer was on the twenty yard line and pickin' up speed.

Chet's horse was kickin' up big divots and Chet was leaning forward like an outside linebacker. He sailed his loop and nailed the steer on the fifty yard line. An amazing catch. The grandstands were empty. Nobody saw it but Matt, and he told me, with a faraway look in his eye, that to this day he can still hear the crowd.

BOB
BLACK

OL' DUFFY

Ol' Duff slept in the bunkhouse in the corner by the wall.
  Nobody slept beside him. It was self-defense, that's all

'Cause Duffy was a chorus of expulsions in his sleep
  That sounded like a freight train goin' through a band of sheep!

His sinuses would vibrate 'til the quilt slid off his bed.
  His snores would roar unmuffled like a chainsaw in yer head.

His hiccups crashed like cannons firing off the starboard bow,
  He'd hack and cough and whistle like you'd stuck a bloated cow!

The window panes would rattle. The barometer would drop.
  Our covers started flappin' and the wood stove blew it's top.

Amidst this raucous tumult we could hear him changin' gears,
  He'd belch like bullfrogs rutting, then a new sound filled our ears.

Big bubbles started forming deep within his swollen paunch
  And rolled through him unhindered like torpedoes toward the launch.

We'd lay in apprehension as we listened to the din
  In dread of what was coming when the final guns kicked in!

The new kid was a rookie and because the bunks were tight
  We had him put his bedroll next to Duffy for the night.

He drifted off uneasy what with Duffy's serenade
  But when the cookie crumbled his whole bedroll came unmade!

St. Elmo's fire went dancin'. Radiation filled the room.
  A whoosh blew out the lantern, I heard a sonic boom!

An eerie echo rumbled. I thought I saw a flash.
  The kid sat up electrified, his face as white as ash!

"What was that!" I heard him cry, "I think I'm paralyzed!
  I must be goin' crazy. . . I see stars before my eyes!"

"No, you ain't goin' crazy but the world's turned inside outs
  'Cause Duffy's last contortion blew the roof right off the house!"

THE HELL CREEK BAR

In the Hell Creek Bar by the light of a star you'll find yourself where the cowboys are all talkin' 'bout horses they've rode. The buckers they've known, the times they've been thrown and the stories they tell might cut to the bone . . . long as the whiskey flowed.

And amongst this crew who'd forked a few, they could rally on and ballyhoo and make ya buy a round or two just to hear one more. They'd crack a smile like a crocodile then try to put the truth on trial and all the while their lies would pile like beernut bags on the barroom floor.

They were kinda loud for a Hi-Line crowd, Jordan tough - Dakota proud, where drawin' out just ain't allowed and you better back yer claim. They'd might concede Texans succeed but the bulk, they'd say, of the saddle bronc breed comes from the land of the Sioux and the Swede and proudly carries the flame.

And I learned right quick in their balliwick it didn't even count a lick if you were a bareback man. "That's child's play," they'd sneer and say, "The only game there is to play is saddle broncs 'cause that's the way it is in ol' Montan.

To slap yer hide on a bareback snide ain't nothin' but a dishrag ride. A good cowboy just can't abide floppin' around that way. Ridin' broncs is an eagle's wing, a prehistoric reckoning, a panther's pulse about to spring, a buckin' horse ballet,

Like skippin' rocks or tickin' clocks, an army tank with Mustang shocks, a magnum load with the hammer cocked, a moment caught in time. Suspended there, this purist pair with Casey-Necktie savoir-faire, two poets in an easy chair makin' ridin' rhyme.

And I'll make a stand that a good one can ride through a storm in ol' Cheyenne, a champagne glass in the hack rein hand and never spill a drop. 'Cause he's a strain of the old time chain who'd ear'em down, grab a hank of mane then swing aboard the hurricane and fan'im till he stopped.

"So, how 'bout you? You forked a few?" He meant to let me parlez voo and prove for true I'd been there, too, whenever the flank man pulls. I said, "Oh, well, I rode a spell," but more than that I didn't tell this hard core Hell Creek clientele 'cause, hell, I used to ride bulls!

A COWBOY GHOST STORY

I was sittin' by the campfire pokin' coals amongst the embers.
It was late up in the fall and I was makin' one last round.
The sun had set itself like it was sneakin' off to China,
Not a single steer I'd seen that day and not a track was found.

Through the rattle of the quakies and the night wind's steady breathin',
a sound, or just a feeling seemed to slither up my neck.
I stopped, stock still and listened but the rustling of the mountain
Gettin' ready for its bedtime was the most I could detect.

There was something, some sensation out there set my nerves to skritchin',
And a shiver rolled like itchy fingers crawlin' up my back.
It was thick as muddy water, this vexation I was feelin'.
Then suddenly a cowboy rode from out the inky black.

DAVE HOLL

DAVE HOLL

He was dressed kindly old fashioned with his mohair chaps and pistol
He kinda came in focus as he eyed me hard and long
"Have you seen my arm?" he asked me but his lips weren't synchromeshing.
Then I noticed that this stranger had been sewed together wrong.

You could almost see right through him. His anatomy was murky.
And his members swayed and slithered like a basket full of snakes.
"And I'll need a head - like yours would do," his ghoulish mouth asserted.
"It's mine!" I cried. I tried to bluff though I dang sure had the shakes.

He had a sort of evil grin, was mostly teeth and fragments.
"Don't argue with me, catfish bait, for tonight I'm hunting hearts.
Just count yourself unlucky that I found your camp this evening
'cause I'm doomed to haunt this trail in search of fresh replacement parts."

DAVE HOLL

He was on me quick as lightening
                as his body came unraveled,
I was in a limb tornado
                and was standin' in the eye.
Arms and feet and hands and torsos,
                noses, toes and metatarsals
Flew around me like a cyclone,
                had my time now come to die?

"Off with his head!" the cyclone said. *"Off with his neck and knuckles!*
A penny for your thoughts," he cried, *"A nickle for your brain!"*
The Cheshire Cat, the Wicked Witch, the ghost of the Headless Horseman
All seemed to have supporting roles in driving me insane.

This kaleidoscopic comet swirled above me then it showered
Down upon me like a blanket where it pinned me helplessly.
Thus it held me till I promised I would make a grim donation.
I could feel my body changing as he took the best of me.

I sat up a little woozy as the spector pulled together.
Still unhinged, I wasn't certain what I thought I saw I'd see.
He was morphing right before me like a human biscuit rising
Using dough still sticking to his bones and parts he got from me.

DAVE HOLL

Like the dirty look I'd given which, on him appeared quite natural,
The upper lip I'd sacrificed was stiff and his to keep.
He moved a little easier with the elbow room I gave him
And I'd sung a cowboy lullaby which put his leg to sleep.

As he rode off, he returned to me the backward glance I gave him.
I lay there really not quite sure if he was him or me.
His departure left a silence broken only by the echo
Of the hand that I had promised as it clapped eternally.

WAITING FOR DADDY

"Mama, when's Daddy comin' home? Is it time to worry yet?"
"By supper, darlin'. Eat your Cheerios."

> *He rode out this morning early. Like he does six days a week*
> *I always make him tell me where he goes*
> *'Specially when I know he's headed over on the canyon side*
> *At least I know I'll have a place to start*
> *So in case he doesn't come back I can hunt for him myself*
> *Or go for help if I get faint of heart*

"Run and git your schoolbooks, kiddos! And be sure to wash yer hands."
"Aw Mama, do we have to school today?"

> *If it wasn't for home schooling I might lose what mind I've got*
> *It helps to pass the daylight time away*
> *And I know I shouldn't worry but I worry anyway*
> *Who wouldn't, if they were in my shoes*
> *I've been up those rocky canyons and I've seen those snaky trails*
> *I know how quick a horse can blow a fuse*

"Mama, Cody said a swear word." "I did not!" "Did too!" "Did not!
I only said Ring went to the commode."

> *Oh, thank God I've got these children just to keep me occupied*
> *But still I'm always lookin' down the road*
> *All afternoon I've watched the sky. It's like I'm playin' poker*
> *You don't know how I fear an angry cloud*
> *And the wind gives me the shivers. Never lets me drop my guard*
> *Nothin' like it whispers quite so loud*

"Mama, when's Daddy comin' home? Shouldn't he be home by now?
We wanna ride before it gets too dark."

> *And the hardest time for me I guess is now till six o'clock*
> *I'm nervous till I hear the home dogs bark*
> *But the kids are my salvation. 'Course, they wanna be like Dad*
> *He saddles up their horse and lets'em go*
> *And I stand here by the window thinkin' 'here we go again'*
> *But they're cowboyin', the only life they know*

"Mama, look! Oh, here comes Daddy. That's him trottin' up the road.
He's wavin', now he's comin' through the gate."

> *"See, I told you kids be patient, not to get your dander up . . ."*
> *And learn to wait, and wait and wait and wait.*

31

MY FRIEND JACK

It was a small corner of the earth. Where seven women carried a cowboy to his grave. The spot sits on a small bluff overlooking Boulder Flats. From his burying place one can see the Wind River Range, the Salt Mountains, the pale blue sky and the Green River as it waters the valley floor all the way to Big Piney.

"It's windy up there," one of the pallbearers told me, "but Jack would've liked it."

Jack was a first rate cowboy, hunter's guide, son of Wyoming and paraplegic. The last several of his years were spent in a care center in a small town, 99 miles from the nearest freeway. Flat on his back, unable to lift a hand.

How he lasted so long after he contracted MS is a mystery to me. How one could keep his spirits up with so little hope is hard for most of us to understand. It gives a reality check to the saying, "You gotta play the cards that you been dealt."

But any letters I received or conversations I had with Jack were never tinted with self pity, depression or anger. Matter of fact, most were humorous and clever, even pullin' my leg. They never drew attention to his captivity. He let me off easy. I, of course, was aware or could imagine the orchestrated effort it took for him to write me one simple letter.

But he was in the care of angels.

A handful of beautiful women who nursed him, befriended him, loved him and kept him in line. They did for him all those things that he and I never discussed, from changing his diaper, to adjusting his cassette volume, to holding his hand.

They kept him from living his life inside his own lonely mind.

Their contribution to his well being cannot be measured in the single flash of a winning home run in the bottom of the 9th, the garish announcement of a million dollar contribution to United Way, or the gala winning of an Oscar.

It is measured in pleasant good mornings, endless bed adjustments, uncountable spoonfuls of soup, unhurried conversations and unconscious pats, squeezes, straightenings and kisses.

It is hard to go quietly into the good night. The will to live is a stubborn foe. But Jack finally went. He was carried to his grave by the angels who had watched over him and given into the care of their heavenly counterparts that watch over him now. And, if I might say, since he's a horseback up there and mobile, the new band of angels probably has the tougher job.

THE COWBOY BALL

Blue lonesome is dang hard to handle
  Especially out where the road ends
   So any excuse for a party
Is welcome, and bound to make friends.

Once a pilgrim seekin' some solace
  Staked a claim a long way from town.
   He'd come from the itch of the city
And in six months he'd settled down.

He had built himself a small cabin
  And sat on the porch one fine day
   When he spied a rider approaching.
He saw him from miles away.

The rider said he was up country
  And rarely came this way at all
   But he thought he'd be a good neighbor
By throwin' a cowboy ball.

The pilgrim inspected this stranger
 Who never got down from his horse.
 He looked like he needed a dentist,
His manner was rugged and coarse.

But lonesome can prey on a body
 And the stranger sounded sincere
 "We can dance all night if we want to
Play music and toast the frontier.

We'll eat and we'll drink and be merry,
 I've whiskey enough for us all . . .
 So whattya say, are ya willin'
To come to a cowboy ball?"

Then a look of shy expectation
 Spread across his unshaven face.
 He nervously tongued his tobacco
And scratched an indelicate place.

The pilgrim was mullin' it over,
 "Ya say there'll be whisky and dance?
 And maybe a kiss in the moonlight?"
The stranger said, *"Yeah, there's a chance."*

"So what should I wear?" asked the pilgrim,
 "It sounds like a pretty good do."
 The stranger said, *"Hell, it don't matter,*
'Cause, Pilgrim, it's just me and you!"

NITWIT WISDOM

Nitwits are partial to wisdom that's usually corny and trite
But the worst part of nitwit wisdom is when the nitwit is right!

I's ridin' pasture for Brimhall checkin' for bad eyes and such.
He'd hired this nitwit to help me. He never did like me much.

"You can't be good at everything," said Nitwit, missin' the steer.
I had to agree that he wasn't... good, that is, that much was clear.

I chased the steer and caught his horns I dallied and then I spoke,
"You rope the hocks and we'll stretch him out!" He tried, but it was a joke.

"Here, set my horse and hold the head." We swapped and I roped the hind.
"Now take back yer horse and hold the heels. Don't let no slack in yer twine!"

I got off to doctor the steer and fished for my last syringe
When a hoof lashed out and cracked my hand! Doubled my arm like a hinge!

I stabbed myself with the needle! He kicked me under the chin
Then he rolled me off over backwards drivin' the needle on in,

"Don't let go of yer dally! Damn!" His rope was floppin' around.
The steer stepped outta the heel loop and headed for higher ground.

"You sorry excuse for nothin! You line-bred drizzlin' dope!
I guess you see he's still draggin' my brand new forty foot rope.

"Yer dumber'n boiled gravel. I told ya keep yer slack tight.
Now he'll prob'ly die of pneumonia. "We watched him flee outta sight.

"Well, look on the bright side," said Nitwit. His wisdom cut to the quick,
"The way that ol' steer quit the country he couldn't'a been that sick."

THE SAMARITAN ANGEL

"He's been hurt," cried out the angel, "That ol' counterfeit went down.
I knew that horse was bad news from the start.
Somethin' bad inside is broken. He's just layin' on the ground.
To lose a cowboy always breaks my heart."

"Oh, Father, please forgive me. Can I take back what I said?
It feels like someone's sittin' on my chest.
There's a mutiny inside me that is tearin' off my head.
That pony sure did put me to the test.

Margaret, Margaret! Where's my blanket. Scooch on over here by me.
Who's out there! You ain't foolin' me a bit.
I can hear your chink fringe rattle, step on up where I can see.
That's better. Drag a boulder up and sit.

Yeah, I know my candle's burnin', and I prob'ly should confess,
But I'm mostly missin' Margaret and the crew.
God Almighty are you up there! I have made another mess
And, like always left the cleanin' up for You.

Well, it seems I should do somethin' if that hand on me is Death.
You think a prayer would be appropriate?
'Our Father, who art in Heaven...,' Ah, it's just a waste of breath,
God knows I'm just another hypocrite.

I ain't foolin' anybody. Oop. I feel it comin' now.
Look Mister! There's a bright light over there.
Could you help me off this rock pile, get me on my feet somehow,
It feels like we're just floatin' through the air.

Look! I'm sound as Lee's ol' Traveler. I'm so glad you's passin' by.
You picked pert near the perfect time to come.
How you found me is a wonder. Heaven knows the reason why,
I'm grateful, but just where'd you say yer from?"

"They be comin'," said an angel, "Better saddle up his horse.
He's not the kind to sit around and pine.
His eternity is busy, doin' cowboy work, of course,
And Margaret's comin' someday, he'll be fine."

39

THE DAY THE RANCH CHANGED HANDS

I first met the crew in the bunkhouse the day that we bought the 4 D's.
I'd come in that night after supper and found'em all takin' their ease.
My job was to count all the cattle and stay till the transfer was done.
I offered my hand to the cowboys and asked how the outfit was run.

"My name ees Man'well Palomino. Vaquero. I came here to ride. The boss said ef I wass illegal, I only could work the outside. He put me down there on the desert, at Cow Creek. Eet wassn't a crime. They brought us the grocery on Tuesday an' that wass how we tol' the time. Four hunnred cows. Yus me an' a kid whose name I remember was Yak. Eet wass col'. I wass from Chihuahua but no way wass I goin' back. Jew remember Yak, doan jew, Tombstone? Jew wass here back then, ees for sure."

"Yeah, I's here when you hit the country. You was green as a pile of manure. You couldn't say nuthin' in English. Pore Jack, he'd forgot how to speak. When you guys come in for the brandin' he wouldn't shut up for a week! I wonder where Jack ever wound up. He didn't stay long around here. All I know's that spring I'd been workin' the 4 D's for over a year."

"Hell, Tombstone, that must be a record! The boss says and swears that it's true that you worked more times for the outfit than anyone else that he knew!"

"You stuff it, Mick! You burnt out ol' wreck. You spend half yer life underground. Catlow Rim's been dug up so much it looks like a prairie dog town. All winter you live in that line shack, prospectin' and minin' fer gold. But . . . sure be nice if you hit a vein before we all git too damn old."

"Say, Mister, my name is Phil Duckett. I guess I'm the new buckaroo. You reckon the new 4 D owners will keep the same guys on the crew? When some of these ranches change owners they come in and clean out the place. It ain't no big deal if they do it, it's just that it seems such a waste. Like Manyul, he knows every canyon and Tombstone he knows every cow. Them hay meadows need to be watered and Mick, he's the man that knows how. Even Pete, back there in the corner don't say much and always looks grim. But he's a mechanical genius and nuthin' don't run without him. Besides, he's been courtin' ol' Hazel, the cook that you'll meet in the morn. Aw, now Pete, don't look at me that way. You know I'm jus' honkin' yer horn. Joe Ben's livin' down in the small house. He's young but a real top hand and his wife's expectin' this summer. Her home-grown tomatoes are grand."

"Perdón, Señor. Doan worry 'bout us. But I hope they keep Meester Yim. I tink he's here for twenny-five years. A shame eef they no hirin' him. Thees ranch he knows like the ears of hiss horse. The trails are cut in hiss grain. He can draw any creek or campo from a map on the back of hiss brain."

"Yup, he's a good boss and we know it to put up with misfits like us. They can pick on me about Hazel but Jim is a man you can trust. But let me just point out a factor. The nearest town's sixty-five miles. Not too many men like the lonesome and lonesome don't fit women's styles. The drifters we get, you should see'em, that come in here lookin' for work. Most all of'em runnin' from somethin', afflicted with some kinda quirk. We even get hippies and outlaws. 'Course, buckaroos, they come and go. But, a few of us, we're sorta home here and we just thought someone should know. So keep us in mind when you go back and if they ask how we might do, could you tell'em . . . we fit the country an' put in a word for the crew."

I told'em I'd sure think it over. We shook and I bid'em goodnight.
My bed was laid out at the main house so I walked up there toward the light.
I paused in the cottonwood shadows the moonlight had made in the lane
And soaked up the smell of the sagebrush and the ozone promise of rain.

I could hear the murmur of voices from the bunkhouse there for a spell.
No doubt they were hashin' things over to see if they'd made their case well.
But men like these cowboys, I'd vouch for. Was easy to cut'em some slack
'Cause twenty-one years this last winter, Manuel had been callin' me Yak.

PROLAPSE FROM THE BLACK LAGOON

It came from outta nowhere, like a prolapse in the night.
Which, in fact is what it was, my friends, the cow vet's scourge and plight.
That pudgy pink projectile from those monster movie scenes
Like some whopping giant burrito filled with attitude and beans.

I was soon laid down behind it on a hillside in the muck
While the cowboy shined his high beams from his perch there in the truck.
His rope stretched from the bumper to her front legs tied in haste.
As I wallowed in the darkness like a pig, stripped to the waist.

It was bigger than a tree trunk. It was slick as old chow mein.
It was heavy as a carpet someone left out in the rain.
I tried to gain some purchase as I pressed my fist in tight,
It was like a thrashing porpoise and was putting up a fight.

I got it in a hammerlock. It was like a rabid dog.
I wrapped my legs around it like a monkey on a log.
I pushed until my shoulder disappeared inside the mass
As I scrabbled for a foothold in the mud and frozen grass.

But alas, with one huge effort she expelled me from her grip.
I shot out like a cannon, rolled and did a double flip
But I grabbed her tail in passing and with strength born out of war,
I dove at the appendage like some punch drunk matador.

I lifted her hind quarters, and I swung her side to side,
Then used my head, like smart men do, to push it back inside!
It was dark there for a second, it was hard to catch my breath
But there she lay, my patient I had saved from certain death.

The cowboy rolled his window down, said, "Doc, are you alright?"
He gunned the engine several times. The headlights got real bright.
"I've seen a prolapse done before but never quite like that!"
"Oh, they taught us that in vet school...But I think it ate my hat."

THE DUCK AND RUN OLYMPICS

When the crew came toward the cookhouse Hazel shut and locked the door.
"Don't you even think about it! Looks like y'all been in a war."
And though Hazel didn't know it she was not that far off track
They'd been workin' pasture cattle and them critters could fight back!

All that grass that they'd been eatin' lubricated their insides
Plus those cows were full as dog ticks and a little loose besides
So when squeezed in some tight corner they could aim their guns at will
And bombard that crew of cowboys with recycled chlorophyll.

Now it's only grass and water as you'll hear the pundits say,
But I'm here to tell ya, pardners, their performance on that day
Was a duck and run Olympics, a projectile Superbowl,
A team of Dutch boys at the dike who couldn't find the hole.

Willie got hit when his hot shot caught a big one by surprise.
With one long blast she turned him into split pea soup with eyes.
Big Sam looked like a seaweed when his beard took several shots
And Pedro's fancy brand new hat got covered with the trots.

A broadside fired from point blank range went down O'Malley's shirt.
He emptied out the vaccine gun, she matched him squirt for squirt.
Then Frank got trapped behind a gate and watched with some concern
While the bunch backed up and measured him and each one took a turn.

It was hangin' off their hat brim, it was drippin' off their clothes,
It was in their eyes, in their ears and prob'ly up their nose.
Not a cowboy was untainted, not a dog escaped the muck,
Not a standin' stick, a saddle horse, a whip or chute or truck

Was immune to their propellant. They resembled works of art
Like guacamole statuettes or cow pie ala carte.
Hazel backed'em to the spigot and stood beside the trough,
"I can't clean up your cowboy ways, but I'll hose the outside off."

Sam was lookin' at O'Malley, "Is this what they really mean
When an Irish cowboy celebrates the wearin' of the green?"
"I don't think so," said O'Malley, "but when I see cows eat grass
I'll forever be reminded of that phrase, **'this too shall pass.'** "

JOSÉ AND THE HOODOO COW

We run this ol' cow in the squeeze chute, she rattled and fought all the way
Then rammed a hind foot through the side bars and managed to cow-kick José.

He dropped the syringe he was holdin'. It stuck in the toe of his boot,
'Least, now he's protected from Lepto. He gave her the gringo salute!

She wedged a big horn in the head gate and dang near flipped onto her side.
It occurred to me, not for the first time how nicer she'd be . . . chicken fried.

She thrashed and created a shambles of everything not battened down.
She moved the whole chute off its footing and knocked poor José to the ground.

We finally, somehow, got her captured and squeezed with her head stickin' out.
My job was to check on her dentures. I carefully reached for the snout.

She buried her nose to the hubcaps and watched with her little pig eye
'Til my body leaned into the strike zone then she swung her head like a scythe!

"She's old!" I yelled, as she grazed my ribs. "Hell, you never looked," said the boss.
"Well, check'er yerself!" I shot back right quick, "It could be my eyeballs were
crossed!"

The vet plunged himself to the armpit, in search of a pregnancy there.
I prayed every year she'd be open. If God would just answer my prayer.

"Big calf!" Came the cry from the backside. Like always I drew the short straw.
It looked like another long winter with Darth Vader's mother-in-law.

José and I watched her departing. We'd spent quite awhile with this bunch
And knew that ol' cow for a hoodoo that dang sure would eat a man's lunch.

She'd climb up yer rope like a viper and make a man hunt a new job
And any poor fool that dismounted could wind up on her shish-kabob.

She might grab the lead when yer trailin' or maybe just brush up and hide
But she'd take a horse in the willers so you'd best be ready to ride.

I reminded José how we'd saved her that time she got stuck in the bog.
I lost a good rope in the process, she wallered José like a hog!

"You nearly got drownded, Amigo." "Verdad. Muy mala, that cow.
If we'd have leaved her for the lobos, my foot, she would not hurting now."

The boss was surveyin' the wreckage, "I think this here tailgate is broke.
Say, José, did she git all her shots?" José eyed the boss then he spoke,

"She's missin' the one she's most needing.
La puerca's too much with her tricks."
"You mean," asked the boss, "Vitamin A?"
"Oh, no, Señor, thirty-ought-six!"

COW XTRACTOR

Ladies and Gentlemen! How many times have you been leading your cow down the street and suddenly looked back to find her with a foot stuck in the storm drain? Or taken her to a nice neighborhood tavern only to have her catch a hoof behind the foot rail at the bar and create a scene.

You need **COW XTRACTOR!**

Yes, the genuine patented must-have, bovine tested, ruminant approved, guaranteed not to curdle the milk, fits any finger **COW XTRACTOR!**

Sure, you say, **COW XTRACTOR** will work on small cows like the Jersey-Southdown cross, but what if you're the owner of a 4-wheel drive Chianina-Caterpiller composite with a head like the bucket on a front end loader and feet the size of Humvee rims?

COW XTRACTOR has a solid gold guarantee. Just return the unused portion with an 8 X 10 glossy of your un-xtracted cow and an affidavit signed by a certified **COW XTRACTOR TECHNICIAN** in your area and we will rush Lars Narsveld, our international **COW XTRACTOR XPERT** to your home, farm or place of business with his backhoe and Handyman Jack to consult with you on how to properly xecute the **COW XTRACTOR**. We are awash in testimonials from satisfied customers:

Says Joe in Tulare:

"My cow was stuck in a rut. Get up, eat, give milk, sleep, get up, eat, give milk, sleep.... over and over. She became depressed. **COW XTRACTOR** *changed that. Now she's taking classes at Community College in Interspecies Relations."*

And from Joe in Bartlesville:

"I had a cow that got stuck in the crotch of a pecan tree twenty foot off the ground. Even the paramedics from Nowata couldn't entice her down. **COW XTRACTOR** *saved the day!"*

Yessir! **COW XTRACTOR** can xtract your cows out of: a womb, the nose of a tractor trailer, a mesquite thicket, a well casing, a deer blind, a Chevy Suburban, a snow bank, a pool hall, a bear trap, a Powder River panel, a portable dipping vat, a yard sale, a ten cow pile-up, the neighbor's pasture, the neighbor's meat freezer, hog wire, a flat bed, the Homecoming float, sorting alley, loading chute, poetry gathering, Cabinet meeting or bad relationship. No farm or ranch should be without **COW XTRACTOR!**

As Joe from Okeechobee says,

"I've tried it all from wrecking ball to dynamite and tractor.
But when she's stuck I've had good luck by using **COW XTRACTOR."**

So, there you have it in a nutshell.

Order yours today so next time you won't be caught saying,

"Now's when we need **COW XTRACTOR** *. . . . . .!"*

CORN COUNTRY LANDSCAPE

Corn country landscape - painted late summer - high clouds, heavy with moisture waiting for afternoon to thicken and darken and start raising Cain.

You can see for miles. Brown, green, yellow patchwork pieces of a giant jigsaw puzzle. Feedlots in the distance, their pens spread out like dark blankets on the side of a hill.

On the horizon to the north and south I can count three spray planes circling over the corn like buzzards. They are so far away I cannot hear them.

Closer I can see circle sprinkler lines leapfrogging over the tops of corn rows taller than a pickup and thick as pile carpeting. The stalks stand straight and tasseled. They remind me of a crowd waiting to hear the Pope. An orderly group. Corn is seldom unruly.

The fields of sunflowers are less organized. They are Woodstockers, jostling and stretching to get a glimpse of the morning's performer.

Suddenly I pass a farmstead. Acres of lawn with a butch haircut from the side of the road to the first row of corn. Who mows all this, I ask. A windbreak. Deep green paint by number rows of pine trees and junipers, beautiful, yet somehow out of place.

A fresh tilled field pushes within a few feet of the road. It smells strong, heavy on my lungs. On this humid morning it reminds me of chocolate cake.

I drop into a creek bottom. Cows of all colors lay like mixed nuts spilled on a green carpet. Bleached round bales hunker along the fence row like melting clumps of sticky candy. I follow the pretty three-line power poles festooned with mushroom-like insulators. Proud they are in their orderliness, functional yet outdated. The DC3's of corn country leading me back up.

Two giant 8 wheel jointed tractors sit visiting with each other in a quarter section field laying fallow. Resting? I don't know, maybe just waiting.

More cornfield city blocks. Each row seems to have its seed company sign out front like a mailbox. Mr. Garst, Mr. Pioneer, Mr. Producers, Mr. DeKalb, Mr. Corn States, Mr. ICI.

The next town comes into view. A water tower and grain elevator.

The implement dealer has his monsters on display along Main street. Like elephants in the circus standing side by side, one foot on the stool, one in the air, trunk raised. Lesser implements parked beyond like resting butterflies, wings folded.

I turn left at the one stoplight. Coffee time.

HELPLESS

"I do solemnly swear, as shepherd of the flock, to accept the responsibility for the animals put in my care. To tend to their basic needs of food and shelter. To minister to their ailments. To put their well being before my own, if need be. And to relieve their pain and suffering up to, and including the final bullet.

"I swear to treat them with respect. To always remember that we have made them dependent on us and therefore have put their lives in our hands.

"As God is my witness."

Helpless.

The worst winter in Dakota's memory, 1997. Cattle losses estimated at 300,000 head. And how did they die? From exposure and lack of feed. Basic needs - food and shelter.

Do you think those Dakota ranchers said, "Well, I'll just close down the store and put on the answering machine. We'll wait 'til the storm blows over. No harm done."

No. They couldn't . . . wouldn't.

"Charles, you can't go out there. The cows are clear over in the west pasture. You can't even see the barn from here."

But he tried anyway. Tried to get the machinery runnin', tried to clear a path, tried to load the hay, tried to find the road.

These are not people who live a pampered life. These are not people who are easily defeated. These are not people who quit trying.

But days and weeks on end of blizzards, blowing snow and fatal wind chills took their toll. Cattle stranded on the open plains with no cover, no protection, no feed, no place to go and no relief from the arctic fury, died in singles and bunches and hundreds and thousands, frozen as hard as iron.

Back in the house sat the rancher and his family, stranded. Unable to do what every fiber in his body willed him to do. Knowing that every hour that he could not tend to his cows, diminished him in some deep, permanent, undefinable way. Changing him forever.

The losses were eventually tallied in number of head and extrapolated to dollars. But dollars were not what kept him pacing the floor at night, looking out the window every two minutes, walking out in it fifty times a day, trying, trying, trying.

Exhaustion, blood shot eyes, caffeine jitters, depression, despair....knowing if he only could get to them, he could save them.

Then finally having to face the loss. His failure as a shepherd. That's what kept him trying.

It is hard to comfort a person who has had his spirit battered like that. *"It couldn't be helped." "There was nothing you could do,"* is small consolation. So, all I could say to our fellow stockmen in the Dakotas is,

"In our own way, we understand."

SECOND TIME AROUND

We must sell it, I told Mother, for we really have no other choice.
The price is much too dear to harbor any doubt.
And though I know we'll miss it the time has come to kiss it
goodbye and find another place a little further out.

When the Indians sold Manhattan to a Dutch aristocrat
in fancy breeches for a blanket and a twenty dollar bill
It presaged a corrosion, an urban sprawl erosion
that covets all the fertile ground and overruns us still.

It's not givin' up, I told her, just that we are gettin' older
and besides, the country's really not the country anymore.
We're surrounded by construction that has zoned the mass destruction
of our pastures and our neighbors and our never lockin' door.

Why, just look at that horizon where we watched the sun arisin'
after milkin' on those mornin's when the air was clear and still.
Now the houses clone each other, everyday, it seems another,
as they creep a little closer like a stain upon the hill.

But there's no way we can change it. There's no way to rearrange it that
would suit us 'cause the truth is, they'd plow us underground.
So we take the offer made us, be thankful that they paid us
enough to make a better start the second time around.

And we'll find a place less crowded, where the air is still unclouded,
where the country still is friendly to our kind of pioneers.
Though the homeplace still might beckon, they will ravage her, I reckon,
so we're better off just movin' while we've got a few good years...
And are able to think clearly and can still hold back the tears.

LOOSE COW PARTY

"It's for you," his darlin' told him as he lay back in the chair
For a well deserved siesta.   Ugh, it wasn't really fair.
It was Chuck, his nearest neighbor - did he have to call right now?
Millard took the phone and listened, "Are you sure that it's my cow?"

As if he'd changed his brand last week or something equally absurd
Like the F.B.I. was posing as a member of his herd
Or an alien invasion took possession of his place
And planned to infiltrate the earth as cows from outer space.

But no easy explanation seemed to ease his heavy load
Chuck said, "Better come and get her, she's a'grazin' on the road."
Saddled up, he hit the highway and broke into a jog
With his wife not far behind him in the pickup with the dog.

He could spot the cow's location from within a half a mile
Cars were backed up to the corner, everybody wore a smile.
Helpful tourists waved and hollered, horsemen galloped to and fro
Swingin' ropes like polo players, someone takin' video.

Millard rode into the melee as the cow turned up the lane.
She trompled through the clothesline draggin' laundry like a train
Through the hogwire to the garden, through the hotwire to the corn,
'Cross the rows with corn stalks flyin', laundry hangin' off her horn.

There were fifteen mounted riders rattlin' through the stubble field,
Millard got a rope around her but he knew his fate was sealed
When he felt the horn knot grabbin' and the saddle slip an inch . . .
He remembered he'd forgotten to retighten up his cinch.

He was still there in the saddle but it now sat on the neck.
We should pause and take reflection while we visualize the wreck.
(pause)
Millard peeled off the equine like a dirty undershirt
He was still tall in the saddle when his boot heel's hit the dirt

You could think of water skiing. You could think of Roto-Till
But when fifteen mounted riders mash you flat, it's all downhill
Millard watched from his position in the furrow that he'd plowed
While the cow crashed through the hotwire, disappearin' in the crowd.

There the band of merry revelers in gesture grandiose
Lashed up the draggin' rope somehow, around a solid post.
The crowd began to dissipate. It was over, they could sense
Leavin' Millard to apologize to Chuck about his fence.

Chuck was gracious. Millard thanked him for his helpfulness and such
But it seemed like Chuck enjoyed it...just a little bit too much.
But he really couldn't blame him. When a loose cow wreck occurs
It's a miserable fiasco, less of course, it isn't yers!

NIGHT MAN IN THE HEIFER LOT

I came on just after supper. Boss had fixed a little sheep camp
        with a bed and propane burner so a feller could have coffee in
the middle of the night.

On my first check it was quiet in my bunch of calvy heifers and the
        moonlight made the cedars look like postcards, I was thinkin'
all was good and all was right.

But at ten I found two mamas with their water bags a showin'.
        They were off there in a corner so I left'em to their business
and went back to fill my mug.

In an hour one showed progress. Heifers take a little longer,
        but the other needed checkin' so I worked her to the calvin' barn
and put her in a jug.

Pullin' calves is always chancy like yer playin' slots in Vegas,
        Put yer hand in - pull the lever - double front feet or the head
back, nothin' comin' but the tail.

But tonight my luck was runnin', head and feet were pointin' at me
        so I chained'em up and gently help him make a change of
address. Like deliverin' the mail.

I administered a rub down, swung him upside down a second,
        stuck a straw up to his nostril, watched him fill his lungs un-
aided with his first taste of fresh air.

Then I loosed the heifer's halter. She was quick to start his lessons.
        Soon her baby found the fountain, tail a'ringin', he was suckin'
in his calfskin underwear.

By coincidence I noticed back behind in yonder corner
        that the other heifer also had her baby up and suckin'
and was puttin' on a show.

It was sorta satisfyin'. I admit I paused a minute
        to appreciate life's mysteries, although mostly I was thinkin'
only ninety-six to go.

IT'S WHAT I DO

A cowboy is the way he is because he works with stock.
        He's learned it's best to ease along
        To find the rhythm in their song
        And not to fret if days are long
            'cause cows don't punch a clock.

That separates him from the crowd that keeps a job in town
        That stack the boxes all in rows
        Or bolt the knobs on radios
        But when the evening whistle blows
            they lay the hammer down.

"A job ain't done until it's done," that's life down on the farm.
        To gather those who tend to stray
        To treat the sick on Christmas Day
        And if she needs your help, to stay.
            Until she's safe from harm.

You see, you can't just quit a cow. Sometimes yer all she's got.
        No reinforcements in the hall
        No Nine-One-One to hear her call
        Just you. Nobody else, that's all,
            to get her through the spot.

His calling is as old as time. It is, will be and was.
        Through blizzards, bogs and bob wire fence
        He stands against the pestilence
        And though he feigns indifference,
            he's proud of what he does.

It's done without a second thought by those who tend the flock
        "It's what I do," you'll hear them say
        With no demand for higher pay
        And I believe they are that way
            because they work with stock.

ANOTHER WHITE HORSE

Another white horse just rode by. I guess I saw him comin'
    I felt him breathin' down my neck, I heard the hoofbeats drummin'.
    I've seen 'em pass this way before. They mark the separation
Of mossy horns from yearlin' bucks. Each one's a generation.

I saw one pass at seventeen, at thirty-five and fifty
    They rode by loud and brave and bold or snuck by sly and shifty.
    They had no time to stop and talk or ponder gettin' older
They pushed their elders for a while then pushed 'em off the shoulder.

They stamped their feet and scraped their horns and kept the turmoil brewing
    With no regard to consequence or history they're undoing.
    Another white horse just rode by. The crowd is gettin' thinner.
I've got no urge to follow 'em, I'd rather go eat dinner

And spend my time with folks I love who'd care if I was missin'.
    Where I can tell the things I know and likewise, sit and listen.
    See, time has worn my edges smooth, a temporal erosion,
That keeps me outta useless fights and outta constant motion.

Oh, I still get my dander up and I still tell my stories
    But you won't find me wishin' I could re-ride long gone glories.
    Another white horse just rode by but you won't see me mopin'.
My grandkid's home from school at three... I'm takin' her a'ropin'

COWBOY GRACE

Dear Lord,

    Yer lookin' at a man who never learned to cook
unless you count pork & beans
        And a flowery grace like you'd read in a book
        is really beyond my means
But You can believe I'm a thankful man
though it might be undeserved
        And I'll eat whatever comes out of the pan
        no matter what's bein' served
I don't take it lightly if it's real good 'cause I'd eat it anyway
See, I know there's people, in all likelihood that might not eat today
        So count me in if yer needin' grace said
        and bless those who provide it
The farmers and ranchers, the bakers of bread,
the loving hands that fried it
        But most of all, Lord, we give thanks to You
        'cause we who work on the land
Know how much our harvest and bounty is due
to the gainful touch of Yer hand
        So bless this food and the life we embrace
        and please forgive us our pride
When others with tables a-plenty say grace
for what we've helped You provide.

THE NEW WW

It was a fairly nice day for Cut Bank in early April. A little breeze blowin' off the reservation, the sun about the color of skimmed milk and the creek startin' to show the runoff.

That afternoon Myron had spotted one of his cows with a calving problem. Only one foot was showing. He brought her up to his covered preg checkin' shed where he had installed a new W W head catch.

Since his wife had taken a scourin' calf into the vet's, he called his neighbor for help. Florence said she'd be right over.

When she arrived Myron eased the ol' cow into the crowding pen and started her down the long alley toward the head catch. Florence stood by to lend a hand.

For the sake of you dyed-in-the-wool Powder River folks, I think I should explain the W W head catch. Think of it as French doors with a gap down the center. Except the doors weigh over a hundred pounds each and are made of steel and pipe.

To set the head catch you open the doors inward, part way. Then when the cow's head starts through you swing the lever so that it closes in front of her shoulders. To release the beast you trip the latch and the doors swing open to the outside.

Halfway down the alley the cow stopped and went down. No amount of tail twistin' and bad language could unwedge her.

At his request Florence brought Myron a bucket of water and the O.B. chains. He lathered up and slipped one end of the 32 inch chain over the protruding leg. On examination he found the other foot further back but already in the birth canal. Myron smiled with relief. But remember, God does have a sense of humor.

Myron deftly slipped the other end of the chain around his slippery wrist and dove back in. He grasped the recalcitrant foot with his hand and popped it into position. Miraculously, the cow sprang to her feet and started down the alley. Myron, of course, followed . . . approximately 32 inches behind!

Florence was racing the cow and her attached obstetrician to the head gate. Florence swung the gate open. Too wide. Then she tried to close it. Too late. The cow shot through. Too fast. Followed by the tethered arm. Too bad.

Just as the head catch clanged shut Myron hit it head-on and rang his bell! The procession screeched to a halt. Florence, in a panic, hit the latch and the head catch blew open. Myron was jerked forward and rear-ended the cow. Surprised, she kicked him smartly in the groin! He fell backwards. She laid rubber and whiplashed him into a belly flop!

Across the corral she ran dragging Myron like a locked-on Sidewinder missile. Through the mud and muck he torpedoed. His waist band was scooping up the night soil and pounding it down his pants until his belt and pockets piled up around his ankles.

In spite of the slick sledding Myron was no longer aerodynamic. His drag coefficient was approaching that of a trawler with a net full of moldy hay. The cow idled momentarily and Myron slipped the chain off his wrist. He plopped in the flop and lay like a plow left in the furrow.

The cow jumped the fence and calved unaided fifteen minutes later.

Myron was treated for abrasions on his oil pan and now wears a 16 1/2, 34, 36 shirt.

IF HEREFORDS WERE BLACK

If Herefords were black and Angus were red
    would breeders of Herefords breed Angus instead?
I mean, would the people who bred Herefords first
    be now breeding Angus if things were reversed.

    Or would they be loyal to red, white and true
        To color of cowlick be always true blue?
    If such were the case would they dis all the blacks,
        Tell jokes about prolapse, compare them to Yaks

More suited for saddle or wearin' a yoke
    Than stubbornly breeding until they go broke.
And those of the Aberdeen Angus cartel,
    would they tout maternal endowments, as well,

    Promoting their native resistence to thorns,
        while cursing as mutants those not sprouting horns.
    Just draggin' their sheath through the cheatgrass and burrs
        like leaky ol' bass boats nobody insures.

Debate would rage on like it does anyway
    if South had worn blue or the North had worn gray,
Or if Henry Ford had been Hank Chevrolet
    You'd still be a Ford man... or would you, today?

    So if Herefords were black and Angus were red
        would breeders of Herefords breed Angus instead?
    The question begs deep philosophical thought
        but don't get disgruntled or get overwrought

The breeders of purebreds run true to the grain
    And efforts to change them would just be in vain
And not 'cause they think other cattle are bad
    "I'm stickin' with this one, 'cause that's what Dad had."

BULL FIGHT

The sound of train cars coupling rumbled through the frozen air
  And struck a nerve in some primeval core.
Our horses started dancin', somethin' made their nostrils flare.
  A premonition washed upon their shore.

We push'em toward the clearing as their apprehension grew.
  They snorted and began to steer like boats,
Prancing sideways, rollers blowing, hoofbeats pounding a tattoo,
  Then a bellow! Our hearts jumped in our throats.

"They're at it," said young Cody as the bulls came into view.
  His voice squeaked. Bulls can have that effect.
He glanced around half lookin' for a demolition crew
  The way the lower meadow had been wrecked.

"Take it easy, lad," I told him, "They'll be lookin' for a fight.
  I've seen'em lift a horse clean off the ground.
Stick a horn right through their belly . . . It'll make your hair turn white,
  A skewered horse can make a hellish sound."

Then two bulls as big as boulders banged together head to head.
  It sounded like the closing of a vault.
Tectonic plates colliding, their reverberation spread
  Like tremors from the San Andreas fault.

They pushed with heads like anvils, bone as thick as two by fours
  And circled, each one looking for a chance.
The ground beneath them pulverized, like waltzing dinosaurs,
  Triceratops reborn for one last dance.

It dang sure wasn't pretty, see, one had a broken nose.
  The blood was splattered up and down their sides.
It smelled like when you gut a buck and get it on your clothes,
  A steaming green and red smeared on their hides.

The young bull slid a horn beneath the other's naked flank
  And hooked him like an ax man felling trees.
The old one groaned and faltered, the young one turned the crank
  And drove the aged warrior to his knees.

"Looks like curtains for the geezer," Cody said with no regard
  For differences existing in our age.
"It's the way of things," he told me. "The passin' of the guard.
  The old must step aside and clear the stage."

One last lunge to finish off the ruler now dethroned.
    It smashed into the beefy upturned hip.
But the peckin' order's fickle, no one savvy's the unknown . . .
    The grass was slick, the young bull made a slip

And went down, his shoulder crunching. For a moment he lay still.
    The old bull rose, no longer in defeat.
His shadow fell across his foe but never moved to kill.
    The young bull stumbled quickly to his feet.

Horn to horn they eyed each other. Then the old bull turned away.
    Cody spoke, "I knew he'd finally get him."

"You underestimate," I said,
    "The depth of nature's sway.
        If you ask me, I'd say
            the old bull let him."

OLD BULLS

If our wives had picked their husbands
    With the care we buy a bull
        There'd be a lot more bachelors on the street.
    We'd be bucked up in the willers
        With the other mossy horns
Just waitin' for a straggler still in heat.

They would check us close as yearlin's
    On the lookout for bad eyes
        And notice how we traveled in the rocks
    But thank goodness we weren't cattle
        'Cause a lot of us sneaked by
Nearsighted, deaf and showin' sickle hocks.

If they'd marched us through the sale ring
    As she sat there in the crowd
        And studied us and read our pedigree
    Could she see we might get paunchy
        And the highest grade we got
In heifer satisfaction was a 'C'?

Would it make her any difference
    If she knew we'd lose our teeth
        And slough our hair and let our toes grow long?
    Would her sire evaluation
        Be affected by the fact
When we were born they used a come-along?

And our famed yearlin' libido
    She'd observed when we were young
        A'crackin' horns and tearin' up the ground
    Now occurred about as often
        As a paid bank holiday.
Could she know then we'd all wind up unsound?

'Course, we tell ourselves she's lucky
    To have had a private bull
        For all these years, through all the ups and downs
    But, down deep each cowman's thankful
        That he curled his lip just right
Before she had more time to shop around.

67

THE PROUD CUT HOLSTEIN STEER

I'll never know just how I got that proud cut Holstein steer.
  I'd rather have lasagna fingers wiggled in my ear
Or get caught eating tofu at the Cattlemen's Hotel
  Than spend another minute with that Holstein steer from Hell.

I put him out to grass with some I'd taken on the gain.
  He soon became the Holstein image of Saddam Hussein.
Most cattlemen I know would never make the same mistake
  'Cause steers like him are meaner than a constipated snake.

One afternoon I drove out to inspect this herd of mine.
  The dog jumped out and vanished, but like stink bait on the line
He soon bobbed to the surface like he'd hooked FREE WILLY's tail,
  Behind him, jaws a 'snappin', came the Holstein killer whale!

I ducked behind a sagebrush but the dog jumped in the cab.
  What followed was a battle like this truck had never had.
Imagine if a coal train pullin' sixty cars in back,
  Doin' ninety miles an hour hit a beer can on the track.

I heard the metal crumple, heard the plastic rip and tear,
  I heard the tires exploding, felt things flyin' through the air.
The dog just kept on barkin' so the steer stayed on the fight,
  Then Lancelot came chargin' up to save me from my plight.

This knight in shining armor was, in fact, to put it blunt,
  My wife in her new tractor with a bale spear on the front.
Distracted by the tractor, the steer came to a stop.
  I raced back to the pickup and clamored up on top.

"Up here!" I hollered loudly, "You can lift me with the spear!"
  The steer came back like bad news, but my wife had heard me clear.
But her aim...(I hollered, "Higher!") was a foot or two off tilt.
  She punched right through the truck door and she rammed it to the hilt!

She pulled back on the lever and we all rose overhead.
  I say 'we all' because the steer had jumped up in the bed.
The last thing I remember just before I pulled the pin
  was Holstein halitosis and the roof a'cavin' in.

I'm still not sure what happened. I was knocked out cold as toast.
  I woke up feelin' dizzy, propped against a cedar post.
The dog was lookin' nauseous there behind the steering wheel,
  The pickup...think Titanic, was a mass of twisted steel.

And what about that proud cut, man eatin', truck stompin', dog kickin',
    Never backin' up polled heavyweight Holstein steer from Hell?
    Well, only time will tell.

But with huntin' season comin' up, his fate is cut and dried.
    He's goin' out to pasture with a bulls-eye on his side.

BOB BLACK '98

BUTCH AND CHOPE

Butch has a theory about hardcore *born-to-rope* ropers; as soon as they build a loop and take one swing, it kicks their brain out of gear.

To demonstrate how this theory works he told me about a friend of his. We'll call him 'Chope', for short.

Butch was runnin' a ranch in the wilds of New Mexico east of Las Vegas. He'd bought a set of braymer bulls to put on his braymer cross cows and one of the bulls had turned out to be a bad actor. He'd shornuf do some damage if you cornered him.

It came time to pull the bulls. They gathered 'em in a corral along with whatever cows came along. As they were workin' the cows out the gate one of the bulls kept tryin' to escape. It was that shornuf bad bull.

Chope was horseback watchin' the gate. The third time the bull tried to slip out, Chope, who was tied hard and fast, slapped a loop on him.

The bull turned and thundered back across the corral. Chope pitched the slack and was tryin' to square his horse around when the bull hit the end of the line. All fourteen hundred pounds of him.

Chope's horse had only got halfway around and was sideways to the bull when the slack ran out. He was slammed to the ground! Butch said he could see that nylon rope stretch an extra five feet as the bull was lifted off his front quarters till he looked like Trigger. At that same moment he heard a sound like Mickey Mantle drivin' one over the centerfield fence. The saddle horn had broken off!

The rope with saddle horn attached cracked like a whip and lashed straight for a horse tied to the fence. It just missed a dismounted cowboy and coiled around the horse's pommel and saddle horn. The tail with Chope's horn still attached whopped the horse's butt. The horse bucked loose, breakin' his reins and the bull galloped off draggin' the line.

Butch looked back to see Chope madly tyin' another rope to his saddle through the gullet.

"Whattya doin'?" asked Butch.

"I'm gonna rope him and get my rope back," answered Chope.

Butch stared at him. His broken saddle sat cockeyed, his hat was gone. His poor horse was shakin' like a front row spectator at a rock and roll concert. You could almost hear his ears ringin'. It was like Chope was lashing him to a harpoon.

Butch placed his hand over Chope's and said, "Let's think about this a minute... nobody's dead yet."

IN AND BY

Three brothers ran together on a summer pasture deal.
They'd sort'em when they gathered in the fall.
There was never more than fifty cows and each one had a bull,
Each brother I should say, the herd was small.

Me and Dick would help'em gather. There were calves in with 'em, too
But the sortin' part would make a grown man cry.
The three of them all shoutin' from the alley at the top
While Dick and I swung gates for IN and BY

And THROUGH and BACK and OUT and STAY and HOLD
        and LEFT and RIGHT!
"That's Norman's Charlois cross that just got past.
And hold that little brindle calf, it's way too small to ship.
Dadgummit, Ted don't bring 'em quite so fast!

Bring that one back. Just hold'em all. No, let the Hereford by.
Now, Jack you leave your catch rope plum alone.
Who's cellular is ringin'? Jack put that rope away
And dang it Norman get off of the phone!

Look out ol' ballie's on the fight! Just put'er in with Ted's.
Not that way Dick! Aw hell, she's jumped the fence.
Come back here Jack! She's outta here, you'll never catch her now.
Forget it if you've got a lick of sense!

The black one IN, the bramer BY, the big calf needs a brand.
I b'lieve that's Howard's wayward bull again.
The brand inspector's on his way. George said he'd take a load
So don't be holdin' up these gentlemen!"

It took us nearly half a day to finish up the sort
And load ol' George a half a trailer full.
And finally find Norm's cellular but not till Howard called
To ask if we had seen his wanderin' bull.

And take Jack by the hospital to sew his finger back,
Drop by the sale to watch the market drown
And remember how romantic workin' cattle really is
And why we've all got day jobs here in town.

TWO MAN JOBS

So there I was pulling one end of the wire, patching fence. The strand lay stretched tight in the claw of the hammer which I had balanced against the post, bracing it with my leg. I sighted down the wire, peeking under my arm and raised the wire half an inch... perfect. I took the staple from my lips and set it against the post just behind the barb and reached for my pounding hammer, which lay exactly three inches beyond my grasp. Attempting to grab it I imitated a contortionist trying to bite off his toenail, all to no avail.

I turned to my assistant... Are You Kidding! I had no assistant. Just another case of one man doin' a two man job.

You run the cow down the alley nearly into the squeeze chute, manage to cram a piece of pipe behind her, run around the chute, open the headgate wide to entice her to come forward, close the tailgate, keeping one hand on the head lever you try and kick her through the bars as she sulls up and drops to all fours. I turn to my assistant...

You've got both corner posts of the south side of your corral set and tamped. You stretch your line, dig a hole equal distance between them and stick in the post. You prop it up with the shovel and a cottonwood limb then walk back behind the first post for a sighting.... too short and leaning to the west. You return to the offending post, kick in some dirt, carefully readjust the shovel and limb props, then return for the second of what turns out to be 300 trips back and forth before you complete the job. By yerself.

Two man jobs crop up often, especially when you're alone;
- Hanging a 4 x 8 sheet of floppy paneling to a wall.
- Leveling a cross beam between two uprights eight feet off the ground.
- Peeling your rope off a steer's head or foot in the middle of the pen.
- Or buying every other round at the tavern.

But to our credit we get it done, and by ourselves if we have to.

When I'm asked what my definition of a cowboy is, I reply, "Someone who can replace a uterine prolapse in a range cow in the middle of a three section pasture with nothing but a rope and a horse."

We who work the land are ideally suited to our often solitary calling. We are that wonderful combination of cleverness, belligerence and immunity to pain.

TED'S BIG STEER

Ted and his dad needed some cows to stock their little ranch in Oklahoma, and they needed 'em right away. A local trader solved their problem and injected a couple loads into them.

By fall Ted began to notice one calf that stood taller than the rest. Must'uve had some Chianina blood coursing through his veins. They called him Alf.

They got the big calf castrated and branded and watched him grow like a weed. After several months Ted gathered a bunch to ship. But Alf ducked back. Ted shook out a loop and gave chase.

"Let 'im go!" said Dad, "We'll get him next time!"

Early spring they went to feedin' cake to the herd. Alf was now a yearlin'. Ted kept thinkin' he'd get a rope on him but Alf was too smart.

He'd hang back 'til the truck pulled forward then he'd hit the cake.

"Yer better off just lettin' him go," said Dad. "We'll get him eventually."

Over the next two years Ted became a master of the bait - trap - ambush - sneak attack methods of capturing a wild beast. He actually tricked Alf into a set of corrals only to see him clear the 4 1/2 foot board fence like a hunter-jumper.

His last fall, Alf was big as an army ambulance.

He let himself get gathered with the cows knowing he could escape at will but Bwana Ted had reinforced his alleys making them too high for Alf to jump out of. Ted sorted off all the cows but one leaving her in the alley with Alf.

You could almost hear the chalk squawkin' on the blackboard of his brain. He backed a closed top stock trailer into one end of the alley and opened the tailgate. He figgered he would take both to the sale if both accidentally loaded. Sure nuf, one loaded. The cow of course!

Alf was circlin' like a hammerhead shark in the shallow end of the pool.

Rust and metal filings flew out Ted's ears as he plotted his next move. With Dad's help as a diversion (bait, some would say), Ted snuck into the back end of the alley driving the tractor with the loader bucket six feet in the air. Suspended from the bucket with chains was an eight foot steel panel. It just cleared the sides of the alley.

Ted drove slowly down the alley until Alf was six feet from the open trailer tailgate. Alf was bouncing off the boards and metal. Splinters flew, welds broke, bolts came loose, cannons boomed, flags fluttered, palm trees bent and waves crashed as Alf turned the earth into a whale wallow!

Ted invoked the cowboy spirit and leaped up into the loader bucket. His eyes blazed with fury, his body tensed, his mind temporarily left the scene of the impending wreck. He was almost eyeball to eyeball with the raging behemoth.

Alf paused in surprise. Ted rose to his full height and screamed at the top of his lungs!

Alf tucked his tail and loaded like a milk pen calf.

When he crossed the scale at the sale the next day, he weighed 1750. Brought nearly a thousand dollars. Dad's still tryin' to talk Ted into gettin' some more like him.

HOOT AND A HOLLER

Hoot had a way of keepin' the bubble level. Which ain't easy as it sounds in the cricks and hollers around Ada.

Ol' man Johnson was tight with a dollar bill but flexible when it came to runnin' cattle. Meanin', he turned'em out on his ranch and gathered'em up but the numbers didn't always jibe. He now owned a small bunch of steers that had evaded sale day for at least three Octobers.

He had made several attempts to bring'em in himself. Goin' so far as to enlist the aid of a cowboy or two, five Boy Scouts on three-wheelers, a company of coon hunters, six archaeologists from the University of Tulsa looking for the Oregon Trail, and a water witcher from Fittstown. But, alas, the wild cattle still remained free!

As a last resort Mr. Johnson asked Hoot what he'd charge to gather the critters. "Ten bucks a head," said Hoot.

Hoot showed up with two horses and a truckload of Catahoula Leopard dogs, best cowdogs in the country accordin' to Hoot.

Hoot and Bill saddled up, loosed the dogs and lit out from the corral. Ol' Mr. Johnson saw'em off, then went back to the house.

It took the dogs less than ten minutes to find the strays. The riders could hear the dogs bayin' and cryin' just past the first holler. Hoot an' Bill rode up on the noise. Eight head of three-year-old steers were bunched up together like baby elephants square dancin'! The dogs were runnin' circles around the frightened beasts.

Hoot called off the dogs and he and Billy started the herd down a fence line. They drove'm straight to the corral. They marched through the gates like teenagers in line at a Garth Brooks concert.

Ol' man Johnson ran out of the house lookin' at his watch. "I need to git some dogs like that," he muttered.

Hoot rode up and dismounted. "Eight head," he said.

"How much will that be?" asked Mr. Johnson, sliding his billfold out of his overall bib and slipping off the rubber band.

"Eight head," said Hoot. "That'll be eighty dollars."

"Oh," said Mr. Johnson, "I can't pay that much. It only took you fifteen minutes." He looked over his glasses at Hoot.

Hoot studied him a second, spun on his heels and stepped to the corral gate. He swung it open and with a wave of his hand shooshed the steers outside!

It took ten days for Ol' man Johnson to call Hoot again.

"Glad to," said Hoot.

"'Course, the price has gone up."

MUD SUCKER

"You reckon I kin cut across?" The brand inspector asked.
The cowboy glanced back at the cattle pen.
"If all you got's them overshoes, I think I'd walk around.
That mud done swallered up a dozen men."

Wayne chuckled as he climbed the fence and walked a little ways.
"This ain't so bad if I just pick my route."
His overshoes weren't buckled tight. He took another step.
The left one stuck and sucked right off his boot.

He nearly went down on his face, but got an arm out front.
He threw his clipboard ten feet in the air!
His solitary overshoe looked like a cypress stump,
Official papers fluttered everywhere.

He slowly pointed his left foot down in the overshoe
Then grasped the back to try and slip it in.
His glasses case came slidin' out the pocket of his shirt,
He grabbed at it but only whacked his chin.

Off balance in a three point stance, he wavered back and forth
And watched his pockets empty in a heap.
His shiny brand inspector badge lit on a crusty chunk,
But when he fell he drove it elbow deep!

He jerked his left arm from the mud which skinned his watch plum off.
Then freed his right from where it stuck in place.
It made a sound like someone throwin' up a horse's foot
Came out so fast it slapped him in the face!

It nearly knocked him on his back. His hat flew off his head,
He grabbed but never really had a chance.
His arm was big around as Michael Jordan's thigh,
And heavy as a hippo's underpants.

He snugged the left boot, buckled it, then stepped out with his right.
Uh, that should be, then stepped out *of* his right.
Boot and all. He looked like a flamingo wearin' socks.
He tried to hold the pose with all his might

But gravity was winnin' when the cowboy threw a rope.
It caught him round the waist and pulled him down.
He took a couple dallies and then dragged Wayne through the muck
Until his body flopped on solid ground.

Later standing in the truck wash, they had tried to hose him down,
Except he wouldn't take off all his clothes
Insisting that his long johns stayed but they came off anyway,
Don't underestimate a pressure hose.

"I know you peabrains just can't wait to tell the whole dang world,
Exaggerate until it's one big lie.
But, at least I'll get some sympathy from my sweet lovin' wife
Though I'm not sure if she will laugh or cry.

She's got a sense of humor but a gentle heart as well
So how she'll act depends upon the case
But, I think the odds I'll ever find my wedding ring again
Are less than her a'keepin' a straight face!"

MR. DEWEY'S HOOK & CHAIN

I went out with Mr. Dewey, maybe learn a thing or two.
We motored through the pasture to his cows
Till our path befell a crossing, a trail laid to waste,
Like forty rhinos passed by pullin' plows.

All the sagebrush had been flattened, great big gouges in the earth,
Bits of cloth and hair were blowin' in the breeze.
Mr. Dewey hacked a lunger and then felt of his black eye
Which now looked more the hue of moldy cheese.

"You?" I asked. He nodded, "I was out here yesterday,
I had to pull a calf, came straight from town.
But I used my regular method, what I call the Hook & Chain,
Where I sneak up on'em when they're layin' down.

Then I chain their little foot up, slip the hook into a link,
The big one on the end, you know the one.
Then I put my boot into it, always keep the pressure tight
That way they never get up till you're done."

"A hook?" I asked, "What kind of hook?" From the rubble on the floor
He fished a good sized hay hook from the mound.
It was old as grandma's photos and, no doubt it was hand made,
It looked like some old stirrup that he'd found.

"See, I prop my back against her with my boot there in the hook,
And push against her when she starts to strain.
I get quite a bit of leverage and they never do get up
As long as I keep pressure on the chain."

"I see," I said. Though I didn't. I looked back across the trail.
I could picture what had happened in my mind
When the ol' cow quit the country through the cactus and the rocks
With Mr. Dewey draggin' 'long behind.

"That explains those nasty bruises and that gash there on yer ear,
But what went wrong to sabotage yer plot?"
"I was wearin' city footwear, not my mud boots like I should.
It slipped right through the handle. I got caught.

But you know they never get up, if you keep the pressure on.
I've proven that a million times before.
And I'll show ya if we spot one that's in need of our assist.
I've got the chain and hook here on the floor."

Then I glanced down to the floorboard. He was wearin' Birkenstocks!
"There's one a calvin' now," he said, "just look!"
"So what?" I asked, suspicious, "Well, I see yer wearin' mud boots."
With that ol' Dewey handed me the hook.

MURPHEY'S LAW

"By gosh, that's a new twist," thought Terry as he tightened his collar against the biting wind and stared at the heifer. She was trying to calve standing up! He eased up on her and dropped a loop over the horns.

She stood atop a swell on the high plains of eastern New Mexico. Terry reached her and tied 100 foot of yellow polyethylene waterskiing rope around her horns as well. A safety line so he could at least get within 100 feet of her if she decided to take off in the 300 acre pasture.

Terry was unsuccessfully tugging on the calf's protruding legs when his father-in-law cautiously drove up behind him.

"Got any O.B. chains?" asked Terry.

"Nope, but we could make a slip knot in the poly rope," suggested Dad, owner of the ranch and resident wiseman.

Terry soon had the yellow plastic clothesline attached to the calf's legs. The remainder of the poly rope lay coiled ominously behind these two obstetrical wizards. It snarled and gaped like a rhino trap. "Lemme grab some gloves outta the pickup," were Terry's last vertical words.

He started toward the truck but stopped when he heard the sound of thundering hooves. He glanced back over his shoulder to see the heifer sprinting toward the Colorado border! He felt something move underfoot and looked down to discover his boot dead center in the discarded coils. A microsecond of his life flashed before his eyes just as the nest of yellow plastic snakes tightened around his ankle and jerked him off his feet!

Down the other side of the swell they sailed, Terry tobogganing like a 200 pound ham tied to a runaway buffalo! Dirt pounded up his pant legs as he scooted and skittered along trying to avoid straddling the brush and yucca that lay like land mines in the obstacle course.

Dad, ever the quick thinker, ran to the pickup and took up the chase! He had a plan. He raced alongside the dynamic duo and, at just the right moment, swerved between the heifer and Terry!

Folks. Pause here a moment and consider the possibilities. The pickup's tire could have stopped on the rope. That, in fact, was the plan. But a cowboy's fate works in mysterious ways and Murphey was waiting in the wings.

Dad did slam on the brakes but the rope flipped over the hood and slid down behind the black iron grill guard. Terry, too, came to a stop when his foot wedged between the headlight and the grill guard. His boot came off. The calf popped out and the heifer stopped to sniff her newborn who was struggling to his feet.

As Terry stood at an angle emptying 20 pounds of New Mexico soil out of his boxer shorts, he pointed out the flaws in Dad's plan.

"Well," said Dad, "Heifers that good are hard to come by and you're just . . . well, heifers that good are hard to come by."

THE HALF POLLED ROOTY TOOT

Yer not gonna keep'er, still, are ya Dad? She must be twelve years old.
I reckon she's closer to fourteen, now, and naturally half polled.

You mean she was sired by a hornless bull? No, she's only got one horn.
Which makes her half polled or better yet it makes her half unicorn.

She could be half clam if your logic's right. Clams don't have any teeth.
You're changin' the subject. We're talkin' 'bout horns, one she wasn't be-
queathed.

She could be half deer and just shed one off while grazin' through the wire
And checkin' this eye you might conclude a cyclops was her sire.

Her stumblin' skips like a circus horse, always takin' a bow.
Son, you're overlookin' her greatest trait, why, she's a gaited cow!

A half polled cyclops with teeth like a clam. A gaited cow to boot!
Why don't you start a new registered breed. Call it the Rooty Toot!

Half the pinkeye, more room at the bunk, and easier to ride,
Rooty Toot breeders will flock to your door. Dad, don't you have any pride.

You're only lookin' to find an excuse to keep her on the place.
I'll have you know I make my decisions on cost, in every case.

While you were babblin' and rattlin' on tryin' to vilify,
I decided to keep her one more year, and you're the reason why.

'Cause bein' the practical man that I am, I say, waste not, want not.
See, I saw you give her that Vibrio and I'd hate to waste that shot.

85

WONDERED HOW HE'D TELL HER

The rancher told his foreman, "Looks like things are gettin' tough
The price of calves is deadly, hell, there may not be enough

    To pay the note this winter, I'm already overdue
    What with buyin' that new tractor, shoot, it wuddn't even new

'Course I bought the neighbor's cow herd back when things were lookin' good
Then we had that bout with Anaplaz, which I never understood.

    We buckled down and rode it out but luck weren't on our side.
    You've worked for me for twenty years, you know how hard I've tried.

I'm not worried for my own self, it's Mother and the kids
I don't know how they will take it if they put us up for bids.

    The last two kids were born here in that house where you live now
    We've raised'em right and taught'em all there is about a cow

And now they're off to college to explore a new career
But deep inside they're plannin' to come back and live right here.

    But that's never gonna happen. The writing's on the wall.
    It's what I've always dreaded and today I got the call.

Bankruptcy's hangin' over me. The lawyer says I'm through
I've lost it all. A lifetime's work. I don't know what I'll do."

    The cattle foreman nodded. But his mind was far away
    On doctor bills and braces, pickup payments left to pay.

He glanced up to his furnished house, his kids and wife and truck,
And wondered how he'd tell her. But said, "Boss, I wish you luck."

BOTH SIDES

Yeah, he wished he was a cowboy but just at times like this	*Yup, he's glad that he's a cowboy* *but there's times on days like this*
When he spent the day ahorseback and had time to reminisce	*When he spends all day ahorseback* *thinkin', 'wonder what I've missed.'*
Never thinkin' about Monday, 'bout the real life he led	*Never knowin' if it's Monday,* *if he'll ever get ahead*
Just the smell of sweaty horses and the peace inside his head	*Just the smell of sweaty horses* *and a blanket for a bed*
How he really could'a been one if the cards had fell that way	*How he grew up punchin' cattle,* *had no other cards to play*
But he never had the option he had other cards to play	*So he never had the option,* *it was bound to be this way*
And he sees the hired on wranglers when he passes them the reins	*And he sees the weekend cowboys* *when they're handin' him the reins*
And he almost wants to join 'em but his common sense refrains	*And he wonders, could he make* *it in their life of ball and chains*
So he joins his boon companions and they toast their saddle sores	*But he joins his fellow cowboys* *and they do their nightly chores*
They revel in the cowboy life and forget the wrangler's chores	*Then doze off while the campfire talk* *drifts in from distant shores*
But by Monday they're a memory as he bills another page	*But by Monday he's back ridin'* *and the open smell of sage*
And forgets the car he's drivin' would've paid their yearly wage	*Reminds him he would not survive* *in a weekend cowboy's cage*

THE GYPSY COW

I was just about to cull the cow when the boss sees me swingin' the gate,
"Hold it there, Doc, for a minute yet
'cause I've not quite decided her fate.

There's somethin' about this gypsy cow. She's a world class travelin' machine. She
must have more frequent flyer miles
than the crew on Apollo 13.

She's seen more country than Lewis and Clark
more dogs than the Moorman's feed man
One time she showed up with a trucker and a sale barn tag from Japan.

Neighbors, sheriffs and folks I don't know call me up when she's makin' her rounds.
They find my name in the state brand book
and right quick, see that she's outta bounds.

She's got a few scars from the fences
she's plowed down and broke to get through.
There's a headlight mark on her shoulder plus a few ropin' burns on her, too.

She's had her close calls, that I'm sure of.
More than once she's escaped certain death. One night she came home in a loader
with a Gomer and Schnapps on her breath.

Last fall she was out on the highway and had flagged down a snowbird's RV
and I swear this New Year's I saw her
in the Rose Bowl parade on TV.

She's worse than a tom cat 'bout roamin' and not picky, is what I've surmised.
I never know what kind of a calf she'll have,
each time I'm always surprised.

One year she whelped her a Holstein pup. She's had Angus, Salers and Wagyus
But I'm worried this fall 'cause the man next door
has started raisin' Emus.

I've really no call to condemn her though she looks like the hind wheels of Hell,
So preg check'er, Doc, just for practice,
she's earned it .... and you never can tell."

I put on a sleeve and proceeded. "This is strange," I said, when I could speak,
"I'd advise you get a nest ready.
I feel feathers, two horns and a beak!"

THE RENEGADE COW

Just bring'er on home, the foreman had said
That is, if I found her, of course,
In seventeen sections of canyons and brush
On the back of a nearly broke horse.

Why he even bothered, I'll never know.
She slipped through the gather each year.
I think he was hopin' that I'd up and quit.
To a smart man it would have been clear.

But I saddled up and made for the bluffs,
Think like a cow's how I think,
The creeks had quit runnin', most tanks had gone dry . . .
So I figgered she'd hunt up a drink.

It was hot as a dashboard in Phoenix in June
When the Yellow Man Spring came in view.
I was stripped to the skivies and knee deep in cool,
When the cow come a'amblin' through.

Whether she jumped the highest or if it was me
Don't matter 'cause she broke and run.
I swung to the seat slingin' seaweed and moss
Thus exposing my hide to the sun.

She's pickin' a path while I'm building a loop.
I miss the first five that I throw.
But out on the flat on try number six
I catch as she's startin' to slow.

I lay on a trip and she plops to the ground.
I sideline her right front and rear.
I figger a soakin' will break her to drive.
My catch rope slips off past her ear.

When all of a sudden my piggin' string's loose!
She comes off the ground like a rocket.
For a second or two I'm a'straddle her head
Then she's blowin' her snot in my pocket!

She might'uve been tired but she plowed quite a while
Usin' me to turn up the curl.
When she finally got tired of smashin' me flat,
She left me head first in the furrow.

That night at the rancho I told the foreman
I'd bucked off. The story was cleaner.
"That renegade cow?" he asked kinda snooty,
I just told him that I'd never seen her.

THE POWER PROFESSIONAL PROCESSING TEAM

It struck in late October like a plague of mustard gas.
       It started with a trickle but then soon began to mass
In pens and cattle alleys on the new receiving side.
       The fall run was beginning and there was no place to hide.
The boss said "Git'em processed, just as fast as they come in!
       A crew'll bring'em to ya and then take'm back again."
So, K.T. got three cowboys and headed toward the shed,
       "You shovel out the squeeze chute, Clyde. Juan, come with me," she said.

       They filled a gooseneck trailer with the stuff she thought they'd need.
              "We'll inventory later, right now, all that counts is speed!"
       By eight the chute was bangin' through the second semi load.
              The cattle to be processed stretched a mile down the road.
       Syringes on the fast draw firin' doses of vaccine,
              Hydraulic handles flippin' like a bad pinball machine,
       Blue smoke and buzzin' bee stings from the hotshots and the brands,
              An ear tag like a snake bite, bawlin' calves and flashin' hands,

An implant undercover, some pour on down the back,
       Dewormer for the pore ones, dehorning with a crack.
Release the head, a clatter. Release the squeeze, a pause.
       He bolts, but then the next one is captured in the jaws.
On and on they processed till their hands were just a blur,
       The cattle like a carousel, the headgate just a whir.
Above the shed an aura that so brightened up the skies
       The cowboys bringin' new ones had to cover up their eyes.

       A vacuum was created like a swirlin' whirlwind.
              As soon as one was turned out, it sucked the next one in.
       The final bunch was brought up but when the last one fled
              They couldn't quit, their auto pilot stuck full speed a-head!
       They might have gone forever 'cept the power went haywire.
              The crew walked out like robots whose brains had caught on fire.
       They stood around unknowing, ears still ringin' from the fray,
              So numb they could remember nothing that transpired that day.

But driftin' in next morning came the news of all they'd done,
       Two thousand head they'd processed, caught and treated every one,
Plus, a hundred saddle horses, the neighbor's feeder pigs,
       A pair of tawdry mannequins with English lawyer wigs,
A marching band from Goodland, sixteen greyhounds from the track,
       The local Veterans Color Guard, a llama and a yak,
Assorted order buyers and a great big plastic steer,
       Not to mention one truck driver with a lot tag in his ear.

Reports just kept on comin' from the countryside around.
    The feedlot was a'buzzin' with each new add-on they found,
But Boss, he saw things different, "K.T., what about the cost?
    Them extra ones you processed guaranteed a hefty loss.
We'll never get our money back no matter how we tried,
    Unless you got some brainstorm..."   K.T. pondered then replied,
"I reckon we could bill'em... or, if mark ups ain't a crime,
    Just charge'm twice the goin' rate at reimplanting time."

THE FEEDLOT HAND

Life is just a bowl of cherries to a first rate feedlot hand,
  All the gates swing free and easy, every day's precisely planned.
The boss is always pleasant and lavish with his praise
And when your wife demands it, you get another raise.

The pickup that you're furnished came off the showroom floor.
  The horses all are gentle and facilities top drawer,
The alleys lay so perfect when you're pushin' to the scale
You only need to set one gate then put'em in the mail!

The feed truck drivers thank you and insist you're always right
  And when you have to block their way they're patient and polite.
Plus, loadin' fats is easy though you're tired as you can be
'Cause the truckers all are helpful . . . and say, "Oh, please, let me!"

The barn where they get processed is as modern as they come,
  Every hot shot's always workin', ain't no pandemonium.
The crowdin' alley's built so good the cattle flow like wine.
They almost fairly work themselves, they wait to get in line.

And on those days when rain or dust or snow get in the way
  The boss says, "Take it easy, heck, they'll wait another day."
On holidays like Christmas when you work the extra mile
The overtime they pay makes all the hardship seem worthwhile.

No feedlot cowboy worries 'bout his job security
  They rarely ever lay one off, too valuable, ya see.
I've heard'em say about the boss, "When all is said and done
It's hard to take his money 'cause I'm havin' so much fun!"

Oh, there are days, they'd all agree that go against the grain,
  Receivin' bawlin' weaners in November's freezin' rain
Or checkin' pens in early March is really not that great
When it takes a front end loader just to open up a gate.

But, all in all, they love their work. The way their mufflers smell,
  The Terramycin on their hands, the Holstein steers from hell,
Scoopin' out the rainy bunks, a calvy heifer mess
And the profound satisfaction when you lance a big abscess.

The glamor of their work ensures an application glut.
  Though many hear the calling, just a handful make the cut.
And he puts his heart into it and stays above the mob
  So he don't have to give this up and get a real job.

93

DOG DAYS IN THE FEEDLOT

Well, it's dog days in the feedlot
       now that summer's nearly done
  I been loafin' through the cattle
       but the steers don't suffer none

    They don't need much watchin', really,
         they just eat and drink and snooze
    Like a bunch of fat ol' bankers
         on an all expense paid cruise

We're not gettin' many feeders,
       not since summer took the bait
  Guess the order buyer's coastin',
       I been told they hibernate!

    Half the crew's been on vacation,
         I took mine way back in June
    Whoa! Better ride a little slower,
         I might finish way too soon!

All the sick pens dang near empty,
       'cept a few ol' chronic pets
  So I pull the odd puffed-up one,
       helps to justify the vets

    But mostly I just check the pens
         if there ain't no fats to ship.
    And I do some contemplatin',
         ain't nobody cracks the whip

But my cowboy intuition
       says enjoy it while you can
  'Cause a thunderhead is buildin'
       that will change the battle plan

    When the dog days in the feedlot
         will have finally run their course
    And the fall'll bear down on us
         like she's ridin' Hell's own horse!

FEEDLOT HEROES

Now and then I get to thinkin' I should quit this feedlot job.
        Go and ride with Buster, what's-his-name, his Texas wagon mob.
Maybe move to old Montana, wear them bat wings for a while
        Or do California daywork in the old vaquero style.

I get my western magazines, shoot, I keep'em by my chair
        And I read'em after lunchin', sometimes wishin' I was there.
See, it all looks so romantic. All they do is brand and ride
        Maybe gather up some wild ones, push'em down the other side

While the cameras keep on snappin', set against a scenic view
        Lookin' picturesque and western, quintessential buckaroo.
It's not often that reporters come by here and spend a day
        And the stories that they usually write are mostly exposé

And I really can't remember any artist incidents.
        All the painters that I've ever seen were workin' on the fence.
'Cause nobody wants to see us cowboys dressed in overshoes
        In our insulated covies on a feedlot winter cruise,

Sortin' fats in some bleak alley with the mud up to our knees,
        Shovelin' bunks or treatin' sick ones, fightin' flies or allergies.
I take a little nap sometimes, in my chair there after lunch
        And I dream that I am workin' for some rope and ride'em bunch

Where a roaming photo graffer lookin' for the real thing
        Is dazzled by my cowboyness, the essence of my being.
And he poses me majestic by the River Babylon
        Mounted on my paint caballo, conchos glistening in the sun.

But at five till one I waken with the image in my mind
        Of the picture he has taken for the cover, but I find
I'm portrayed in all my glory standin' in the chronic pen
        Lookin' at a scruffy lump jaw that needs lancin' once again.

I get up and grab my jacket that's the color of manure
        And I head back to the feedlot, catch some horses for the shoer,
But I worry if my heroes in that cowboy magazine
        Ever get a lick of work done, 'cause they always look so clean.

THE GRAPEVINE

How better to impress his new lady friend, thought Rob, than to take her to his friend's rancho for an afternoon branding and BBQ.

She would be pleased to see that he had many friends who drove pickups with chrome grill guards, tinted windows and coordinated paint jobs. He admitted to himself that his own outfit was less ostentatious. His '64 model two horse trailer had been repaired so many times that it looked like a well drillin' rig! The '76 pickup was using 2 quarts of oil to a tank of gas and his horse was . . . well, ol' Yella looked right at home.

Rob was eager as a piddlin' puppy when he picked up Delilah and headed north outta the Los Angeles area. He was anxious to make a decent impression but one large obstacle lay in the pit of his stomach like a pea in the Princess' mattress . . . THE GRAPEVINE! It was a monster of a hill dreaded by truckers and people who still drove a Chevy Nova.

The engine was screamin' and smokin' like a burnin' pile of creosote posts when they finally leveled out at the summit of the Grapevine. Rob had sweated through his shirt but he sighed with relief as he gave Delilah a comforting look. She smiled back uneasily. Then the motor blew! A big dent appeared in the hood and it sounded like someone had dropped a Caterpillar track into the fan!

They coasted silently into a service station at the bottom of the grade. He assured his sweetheart there was *"no problema"*. He had lots of friends nearby. Her reaction was one of forced optimism.

By dark he'd borrowed a pickup from Hank and they both agreed returning back home was the best option. He loaded Yella, hooked up the trailer and back over the Grapevine they flew! Halfway down Rob managed to slip his arm behind Delilah's neck. Soon she was lulled into discussing her dreams of home and family. She snuggled closer as he watched a tire bounce by him on the driver's side. No headlights shown in his rearview but he couldn't help but notice the huge rooster tail of sparks spraying up from beneath his trailer! He could see her astonishment in the flickering light.

Rob wheeled the screeching rig to the shoulder. Together they unwired the trailer doors and Yella stepped out, unhurt. Rob tied him to the highway fence and unhooked the trailer. Rob's facial tic had returned.

Seemingly in control, he jumped in the pickup and headed south for the nearest phone to borrow a trailer. He returned to the scene to find Yella grazing in the median with semi's whizzing by on both sides and his date shivering over the still warm axle, forgotten. She, herself, was smoldering. She spoke not a word and Rob conceded to himself that it was gonna be hard to regain her confidence.

In the space of 12 hours and 50 miles he had left his pickup, his trailer, his horse and his girl scattered from one end of the Grapevine to the other.

Next day he towed the pickup to the shop. He left his trailer to be impounded by the State Police. His horse made it home safe but Delilah changed her phone number, wrote him out of her will and has not been heard of since!

THE YELLOW RIBBON

The woman stood in line. Her eyes stared vacantly. Her face was gaunt. A thin film of dust covered her clothing. The weight of the world lay on her shoulders. She was muttering under her breath. A fly touched her cheek. She brushed it off, unthinking.

"So, how's it going?" I asked, interrupting her quietude.

"Clint just showed his pig, Tanya can't find the sheep clippers and Justin's rabbit was disqualified 'cause it had a black toenail."

"How much longer you think the hog judgin' will go on?" I asked.

"Ten or eleven. Who knows? It doesn't matter because we've got to be here to close the petting zoo for the night."

"Look out!" I shouted as a loose pig shot by her blind side followed by a sweaty boy with sawdust on his pants and a number flapping on his back. She didn't pay it any mind. She looked past me.

"Tanya. Where have you been? I told you to check with me at 8:30. You need to work on your lamb . . . I don't know who has the clippers. Borrow somebody's. Where are you going? You check with me at 9:30!" The last two sentences were spoken to her daughter's disappearing back.

She turned and spoke to the two kids manning the Purple Circle 4-H Club Food Booth, "How's the ice holding up? Set out more cups."

I drifted back to the bleachers to watch the hog judging. It looked more like kids and pigs at the Ice Capades! Only a parent would be able to match the careening swine with their pursuing herdsman.

I saw the judge pick his way through the melee and award a purple ribbon to a beaming teenager. The man next to me applauded. "Your daughter?" I asked.

"No," he said. "That's mine in the red shirt with the Hamp. She really tried, practiced showing him at home for weeks. He needed a little more weight, I guess. I know she's disappointed but I'm proud of her."

I spotted his daughter. She stood with great dignity near the fence, pig at her side and watched the ribbons being passed out. She looked to be about ten. In time the judge approached her and handed her a yellow ribbon. She broke into a wide grin, reached down and patted the pig.

Dad nearly knocked me off the seat with his clapping!

"Congratulations," I said after he settled down.

"Yeah," he said with a silly smile on his face, "That's what county fair is all about . . . kids."

MY KINDA TRUCK

I like a pickup that looks like a truck
    And not like a tropical fish.
Or a two-ton poodle with running lights
    Or a mutant frog on a leash.

Give me one tough as a cast iron skillet
    With a bumper that's extra large
And a hood that weighs over eighty-five pounds
    And looks like the prow on a barge.

I like style but since when should a truck
    Be touted for comfort and ride.
Power windows on pickups? Reminds me of jeans
    With a zipper that zips up the side.

They should soak up the dents of everyday life
    Like a boxer losin' his teeth.
And I like a truck, when you lift up the hood
    You can see the ground underneath!

Pickups are kinda like welding gloves.
The pock marks are part of the deal.
Not pretty, just built to get the job done
Like the dummy behind the wheel.

Don't get me wrong, I know beauty's skin deep
And ugly is in the eye,
But to find out if your truck is my kinda truck
Here's a test that you can apply:

If you have a small wreck in the parking lot
By backin' a little too far,
Your only worry is how big a mess
You made of the other guy's car!

Photos: Matt Cook

THE FAIRBOARD

It was every fairboard's nightmare when the lightning hit the stage.
'Course, it might have been expected; it was just another page
In a trail of disasters that befell our county fair
That began when Dr. Knockwurst told us we should be aware

That a stomatitis outbreak might shut down the rodeo
Not to mention all the entries in the Junior Livestock Show.
Then the day before we opened they began to excavate
Down the center of the highway that runs up to the main gate.

Of course, they hit a waterline. We were Lake Louise by dawn.
But no water in the spigots in the barns or in the john.
So we planned on shuttle parking using pontoons and canoes
But we finally wound up asking folks to just take off their shoes.

And the carnival got testy 'cause we couldn't build a bridge
Plus the vendors all were grumblin' due to decreased patronage
But the tractor pull went okay 'cept they pulled a light pole down
Which played havoc with the dog trials when two handlers almost drowned.

On the morning of the last night the promoter called to say
That the singer had a sore throat and could not perform, no way.
But by noon it didn't matter 'cause the clouds came rollin' in
And the crowd all left in lifeboats so by five we pulled the pin.

We retreated to the office down beneath the grandstand seats
Where the fairboard did its business and hashed out the balance sheets.
'Cause tonight we were survivors. Like a pile of used retreads
Only glad that it was over, all we did was shake our heads

And ask ourselves why anyone would take this thankless chore
When a kid, in tow with mother, stuck his head in through the door.
He had lost his yellow ribbon, she explained, both drippin' pools,
And wondered if by some small chance, if it weren't against rules...

Could we? "Course we could!" I shouted.   "We're the fairboard! That's our thing!"
So we picked him out a dry one. It was like we crowned him king.
And he tried to say his thank you's but his tears got in the way.
Time stood still as he departed. No one had too much to say

'Til the lightning hit the stage lights, then I heard me volunteer,
"I reckon we should get them fixed 'fore we do much else next year."

103

BALIN' WHEAT

Glen said J.T. liked old pickups, too. But sometimes they had a mind of their own.

Early one summer morning J.T. loaded his good dog, Sam, and headed down to the wheat field. It had been cut and he planned on balin' some wheat straw as long as it still held the dew.

It was a fine western Kansas mornin'. J.T. made two passes around the wheat field before the sun burned off the moisture. He parked the 930 Case with the New Holland round baler and decided he could make it to Winona just in time for coffee shop communion. He leaped aboard his '79 Ford 4-wheel drive and cranked the engine. Unfortunately, it didn't crank back!

Starter problems, he knew. It had happened before. Something electrical that required a little short circuiting wizardry. He raised the hood. Sam lay under the tractor in the shade waiting for his command to 'Load up!'

J.T. had no manual choke so he wedged a shotgun between the seat and the foot feed. Diggin' through his Snap On hi-tech tool kit, he fished out a fence stay and a pair of pliers. He shorted the faulty electrical connection. The starter kicked over and the engine caught. It was at that moment that J.T. realized the old '79 was in gear!

It lunged into motion! He slammed down the hood and dove out of the way! Out across the wheat field it chugged, pickin' up speed! Sam, the dog, came out from under the Case tryin' to jump in the back, but it was goin' too fast!

Down through the stubble it rumbled followed by dog and man in hot pursuit! The ol' pickup displayed an unerring sense of direction and seemed to navigate itself through the bogs, rock piles and round bales. On several occasions when it was slowed by a mud hole or steep rise, it looked like Sam might catch up. But the pickup had lots of pasture experience and always managed to elude the pore ol' dog, who thought he was bein' left behind!

Finally it nosedived into a washout, knocking the twelve gauge out of position and died a natural death.

J.T. followed the tracks and found it face down up against the bank. Sam was in the back where he belonged, but breathin' heavy.

J.T. eventually made it to the cafe around noon to tell the story. But everyone said it sure gave new meaning to the term "gunning the engine!"

OLD TIMES

He was just another geezer with a weary repertoire.
The kind you find most afternoons in a beery western bar.
I's comin' back from Spanish Forks where I'd been up to the sale
When this sign reached out and grabbed me. It said, **We serve beer and ale.**

    It was dark inside and shady, though it wasn't really cool
    But it beckoned like a siren so I sat me on a stool.
    "A beer," I said, then looked around at the piddlin' crowd wuz there.
    A couple cowboys from the Rez and a lot of empty chair.

The geezer leaned against the rail with a whiskey in his hand.
For small talk I threw out a line, "Do ya recognize that brand?"
"Which one?" he finally answered back. I was starin' up above,
"That big Bar V there on the wall." *"Sonny, I kin read it through a glove.*

    I could spot them cows for half a mile. Say, where'd you say yer from?"
    "Near Springerville," I answered back, "I been order buyin' some.
    But back about six years ago I was on the Bar V crew.
    I worked for Mr. Blankenship.   Finest man I ever knew."

"You mean Red Butt Blankenship! Had a tooth gone in the front?
Yer tellin' me he runs the ranch! He weren' nuthin' but a runt!
He couldn' even hitch the team less you showed him how each time.
And givin' him a good reined horse wuddn' nuthin' but a crime!"

    "There weren't no teams when I was there." I could feel my hackles rise.
    "Mr. Blankenship said that tractors were the best farm compromise.
    I worked for him till late last year and he taught me quite a lot.
    The neighbors all respected him and put stock in what he thought."

"Well, he dang sure was a thinker. He put off more than he did.
You had to show him everything! Like a puppy or a kid!"
I was gettin' irritated with his disrespectful smear,
"Well, they honored him in Salt Lake at the Cattlemen's last year.

    Now he travels quite a little since they made him president."
    "Anything to keep from workin'. That's the way he always went.
    He was crazy as a bed bug! 'Specially when he had a drink."
    "Mr. Blankenship's a bishop! Yer mixed up is what I think..."

"Hell, I've seen him moon the coyotes wearin' nothin' but a sheet!
'Less he changed since I once knew him, look behind his pickup seat!"
I asked, "How come you know so much?" He said, *"Sonny, I was there.*
Who ya think called up the coyotes. Back then we was quite a pair.

106

If yer wonderin' 'bout his nickname, I was there to share his grief.
You just ask him 'bout a pit stop and a stingin' nettle leaf!"
He offered me another drink but I said, "I gotta go."
"Nice to visit with ya kid," he said, *"and tell Red Butt hello."*

"Who are **you**?" I asked the geezer.   "Me? Just one of his old pards.
But if you see that Blankenship, tell him Old Times sends regards."

MOONRISE

I didn't have time to watch the moonrise over the mountains last night.

I'd gone out to get something and noticed a glow on the silhouette of China Peak. 'A fire,' I thought. But it was still too wet for timber or brush to be burnin'.

Then, as I watched, the curve of the moon tipped over the rim. It was golden as an egg yolk and lit the sky. "How beautiful," I said aloud to myself. It continued rising...declaring itself so fast you could almost see it moving.

I heard the horses bang the feed tub. I walked over and peeked into the corral. They gave me the eagle eye, ears up. I'd just shod the new horse and quicked his right front a little. He was standin' on it square. I felt a little lighter.

I glanced back at the moon. The top third sat on the jagged edge of the earth's incisors. It was sneakin' up on the valley.

I stared a moment. 'Somethin' that big ought to be makin' a sound,' I thought. Like a rumbling locomotive or a creaking timber. Maybe the moaning of hi-line wires in a windstorm. I listened. Nothing but a nightbird and the distant humming of a truck on the highway.

I found the feedtag I was lookin' for and stuck it in my pocket. Too late to call the feedstore tonight but I'd have it ready when I called the next morning. Then I remembered I'd promised to call the neighbor. He wanted to borrow the brush hog soon as I was done with it. I'd finished that afternoon.

I quickstepped back to the house. As I crossed the drive I noticed the lane was dark but the tops of the trees were sparkling like they'd been sprinkled with glitter. "Man," I said to myself, "It's too bad some photographer isn't here to capture this incredible picture. No one would believe it was real."

I stepped up on the porch, made a mental note to fix the railing that was hangin' like a broken arm, and opened the screen door. I held it a moment and looked back to the east. The dogs watched me hesitate, thinkin' I might not be done outside.

The moon shone like a yellow headlight waist deep in a pool of dark water. Gonna be full tonight, I thought as I walked in the house and made for the phone. The screen door slammed behind me and my lost opportunity.

I didn't have time to watch the moon hang itself in the sky. A scene so timeless it has been watched by Neanderthal men, Pharaohs, Moses, Michalangelo, Columbus, even Pancho Villa and Garth Brooks.

But not me, I didn't have time. I had to make a call.

OF THE LAND

We are of the land. The land that everybody's tryin' to save.
  We are of the earth. Of the earth from the glimmer to the grave.
We're the plankton in the ocean, we're the grass upon the plain,
  We're the lichen on the tundra, we're the clevis in the chain.

You will find us on the outskirts coaxing bounty from the ground
  With our watchful eyes cast skyward, well beyond the lights of town.
Dust to dust we are committed to the earth in which we stand,
  We are farmers by our birthright, we're the stewards of the land.

There are those who sit in towers who pretend to know what's best.
  They pontificate and dabble. They bray loudly. They protest
That a peasant can't be trusted with the land to which he's bred
  And they rail with the courage of a person who's well-fed.

We have labored through the ages for these power hungry kings.
  We have fueled the wars of nations with their arrows and their slings,
We have fed the teeming masses with our fish and loaves of bread
  So the poor would sit and listen to the words the prophet said.

Mother Earth can be forgiving when, in ignorance, we err.
  But she can die of good intentions. She needs someone who will care.
Not with platitudes of poets touting blood and sweat and toil,
  But the daily care of someone with his hand upon the soil.

Though the bullets become ballots and the rulers change their name,
  They will still march on their bellies, so our job remains the same.
For the bureaucrats and battleships, the Einsteins and the choirs
  Would spend their life behind the plow, if no one fed their fires.

WATER

The big boy land developers hired them a worn out hack
　　　To go and buy the water rights off farmers down the track.
　　"Just pay 'em anything they ask. Hell, any price on earth.
　　　Those farmer's haven't got a clue of what it's really worth."

"Them's fightin' words," the farmer said. *"This water ain't for sale.*
　　　It's all that keeps this place alive. Without it crops would fail."
　　The lawyer sorta laughed it off. "We'll get it anyway.
　　　The cities need it all to grow. You can't stand in their way.

It's progress, you should know by now you can't hold back the flood."
　　　"There's lifetimes given to this land. The water's in their blood."
　　"Old man that's ancient history, besides we'll make you rich.
　　　Just name yer price, you'll have it. It's nothin' but a ditch."

"Yer hollow as your vacant eyes. Yer empty as yer word.
　　　You can't see past the dollar signs. These things that you've inferred
　　Are bigger than yer lawyer's fee, yer Judas ten percent.
　　　You've no respect for anything, you covet just the rent.

Go back to your rich puppeteers who've never broke a sweat,
　　　Who ride in when the battle's done and use their bayonet
　　To finish off the wounded brave and pick their pockets clean
　　　Then sell their spoils to innocents to keep their cities green.

Explain to them the difference between value and price.
　　　That value isn't what is paid it's what is sacrificed
　　That gives it worth. It's measured in the turns around a field,
　　　In families and community, in broken bonds and healed,

In barns burnt down and harvest lost and kids gone off to war.
　　　Explain to them it's measured in grooves worn in your soul... or,
　　In depths of neighbors breaking hearts when someone's lost a wife,
　　　And that you can't just set a price on someone's way of life.

SHOEIN' PIGEYE

"Just count me out," said Wilford as he lay there in the dirt,
    A shoein' rasp behind his ear, a hoof print on his shirt.
        "I'll handle this," said Freddie, **"You jus' git outta the way.**
        This sorry bag of buzzard bait has met his match today."

The horse weren't much to look at, just the kind a trader'd buy
    But you knew that he was trouble when you looked him in the eye.
        It was small and mean and glittered, as deep as Jacob's well,
    Like lookin' down the smoke stack of the furnace room in Hell.

Freddie grabbed a set of nippers and bent to grab a hoof.
    When he woke up... his shoein' chaps were danglin' from the roof.
        His shirt tail hung in tatters and his watch had come unwound.
    The nipper's orbit finally peaked. They clattered to the ground.

"Go get a twitch," said Freddie, **"I'm about to clean his clock."**
    He tied a rope around his neck and fished it past the hock
        Then pulled back on the sideline to instill a little fear
    When Pigeye bit a good-sized chunk from Wilford's offside ear.

Wilford tangled in the sideline and tried to navigate
    Whilst draggin' 'round the horse corral like alligator bait.
        Freddie tried to stop this trollin' with a loop around the head,
    And it might'a worked if Freddie'd only roped the horse instead

But, of course, he caught pore Wilford, who left a funny track...
    Sorta like an oil slick, when Freddie jerked the slack.
        By now the boys were testy and tired of this travail
    They figgered they'd be done by noon but they'd not drove a nail.

"Go git the boss's Humvee! We'll winch him to a post."
    They got the cayuse necked up tight, and set to work... almost

'Cause the halter broke and Pigeye walked the length of Freddie's back.
    They rolled beneath the axle like two lovers in the sack.
        Freddie heard the sound of gunfire like a thousand amplifiers,
    "I've got the sucker pinned down, Fred, I shot out all the tires!"

It was dark when Wilford stood up and laid his hammer down.
    A gross of crooked horseshoe nails lay scattered all around.
        The place looked like a cross between the tomb of Gen'ral Grant
    And a Puppy Chow explosion at the Alpo Dog Food plant!

Wilford couldn't move his elbow but he grinned and proudly said,
"Ol' pard, we done a good day's work,"
to what was left of Fred.
Freddie crawled out from the wreckage
and staggered to one knee,
"What say we wait till mornin'
to put on the other three...?"

MISTAKEN IDENTITY

Is this the horse I think it is? You had him here last year.
That rope got tangled in his feet, he jumped just like a deer.
He pulled the brandin' pot plum down and hung up in the gate.
It tore clean off its hinges which is why it don't hang straight.

I'm tellin' you I know this horse. He threw you cross the fence!
The ground crew tried to find a hole and hide in self-defense
He bucked back through the cows and calves and tried to kill Joe's truck.
I've never seen a grill fall off, ol' Joe was thunderstruck.

He finally stopped to catch his wind, his hide was wringin' wet.
We tried to slip up next to him, as close as we could get
To try and grab a draggin' rein was all that we could hope,
But he nearly did a back flip when Jim Bob shook out a rope.

I thought that net wire fence would hold but I sure missed my guess.
He climbed it like a Sherman tank and lit out toward the west.
The whole corral was tore up bad, we've fixed it back since then
But there's still bite marks on the gate inside the brandin' pen.

You sure you wuddn't here last year, performed that tour de force?
"You've got me mixed up with someone, hell, I just bought this horse."
By gosh, ol' Son, I think yer right, you wuddn't even here.
It seems like I remember now, Slim rode him here last year.

he sang . . . .
'little Joe the Wrangler'

The dry grass crackled underfoot,
was dang near stirrup high
The horse and rider left a wake
as they went riding by
Their shadow swam beneath the horse,
no elbows stickin' out
The hoppers thick as dirt road dust,
the prairie sick with drought

No cattle in this section piece. They stayed down by the creek
The rider only rode to see how bad it was this week
Due east across the grassy sea he rode with squinting eyes
No cloud to break the baking heat, but then to his surprise

The slightest shadow fell across the ground on either side
He stirred from somnolescent thought, from soporific ride
His senses came alert and he sat straighter in the seat
The blue sky had a pinkish tinge . . . and then he felt the heat

He swung his horse back to the west and saw the wall of flame
The god of fire was hot to trot and back to stake its claim
It felt like his whole head caved in as blood drained from his brains
The fist of fear that gripped his heart squeezed dread into his veins

They wheeled as one and in two jumps were flying 'cross the plain
They ran flat out for near a mile but hardly did they gain
For now the fire was like a mob that fed upon its own
Self-conflagrating cannibals cremating flesh and bone

The smoke was in his horse's nose,
the fear was in his eyes
The froth blew off
his heaving flanks
and soon was vaporized
A hole, a hump,
a hidden clump,
whatever . . . jammed the gear
The horse went down
like he'd been shot
The rider
landed clear

The flames hung down like curtains
there behind the fallen horse
The beast was struggling to his feet, the wind was gaining force
The rider dug a wooden match from out his sweaty shirt
And struck it on his zippered fly, then reached down to the dirt

And lit a clump of tinder grass without a second thought
In moments with the steady breeze the helpless prairie caught
The horse in panic tried to run but couldn't bear his weight
His right hind packed up under him. The rider didn't wait

He peeled his shirt off with a tug and quickly tied a blind
Around the faunching horse's head to try and calm his mind
The spot he'd lit was fanning out but in its wake lay bare
A blackened smoking patch of ground that beckoned to the pair

With coaxing-pulling-pounding will he danced the horse around
Until they stumbled through the ring and stood on burnt-off ground
He jerked his rope down from the horn and, talking all the time
He sidelined up the good hind foot to drop him on the dime

Then pulled him down and dallied up and somehow with the rest
Reached down and looped the left front foot and pulled it to his chest
He looked up at the raging fire that towered overhead
The wind that beat hard on his face
now pressed his back instead

The fire was sucking oxygen
to feed its hungry forge
The backdraft fueled the dragon's flame
that bore down on St. George
With nylon rope and reins in hand
the rider cuddled near
He lay beside the stricken horse
and sang into its ear

...He's Little Joe the wrangler, boys... the fire became a roar
It rose up like a cobra's hood *...he'll wrangle never more...*
The sky turned black *...An OK spur from one foot lightly hung...*
The devil's furnace set on high but still the cowboy sung

...The boss he cut him out a mount... like bugs caught in a yawn
They lay in the volcano's throat *...and kindly put him on...*
Surrounded by a ring of fire, they clung to their domain
Two captives on a railroad track beneath a passing train

...He's ridin' ol' Blue Rocket with a slicker o'er his head...
The peak of the inferno was enough to wake the dead
The rider tugged the shirt on down to wrap the horse's nose
His voice raw, he whisper-sang and kept his own eyes closed

...But one of us was missin', boys... by now he'd worn a groove
Together there, just mouth to ear the pony never moved
...Next mornin' just at daybreak... then the wind began to turn
The rider felt a different breeze, his cheeks began to burn

...Beneath him mashed into a pulp...
still trapped in his own hell
The rider croaked his scraping dirge,
...His spur had wrung the knell...
How long he held the horse's head
no one could really know
And on he sang
*...Our little Texas stray
poor Wrangler Joe...*

The pilot finally spotted them and radioed the ground
    The boys who reached him in the truck weren't sure what they had found
The horse was layin' on his side his head a'pointin' north
    The rider hunkered over him just rockin' back and forth

        The tee shirt burnt clean off his back, his bare head fairly scorched
          The horse's hair was singed like wool, his mane and tail torched
        The pair smelled like a brandin' fire but what disturbed the boys
          Was comin' from the rider's lips, a scratchy humming noise

A raspy ragged lullaby that carried on the air
    And slithered up their prickled necks and held 'em frozen there
Before them grinned the face of death, the Earth, its skin unpeeled
    The world consumed by fire this time, Apocalypse revealed

        But beating in this ruined place two hearts somehow prevailed
        And hung in balance by a thread . . .
           a sigh could tip the scales
           Then Jim eased up,
            like you would do a spooky colt, perhaps
          And touched him with an outstretched hand . . .
             the rider just collapsed

                ***

          This tale was told in countless camps
            where killin' time's the rule
               Some say the rider was insane
                 and babblin' like a fool
         But Jim, who reached the rider first
          was haunted his life long
             With **Little Joe the Wrangler...**
               But, who knows . . .
                 it's just a song

DUNNY AND THE DUCK

There are strange tales told in the days of old
when cowboys tested their luck
But the queerest portrayal of life on the trail
was when Dunny ran off with a duck.

The boys and I were drivin' steers up north and stopped at Hymer
To rest the bunch and have some lunch and just restoke our primer.

We tied our horses to the fence, commenced to tellin' whoppers
And thus inclined, we watched a line of ducks come huntin' hoppers.

Those ducks fell in behind our steeds and sorted through their droppings
For bits of grass or oats they'd passed like barnyard fowl out shopping.

Young Orville hefted up a duck which kinda starts this caper.
Behind unfazed, ol' Dunny raised his tail to break a vapor.

Why people do the things they do remains a constant wonder.
Like Orville there, saw tail mid-air and stuck the duck up under!

To say it took his breath away would sure describe ol' Dunny
And just as true, I reckon, too, that duck was breathin' funny!

'Cause underneath ol' Dunny's tail two wings protruded oddly
And filled the air with flyin' hair the racket was ungodly.

You talk about a hissy fit! Both fur and fowl got ruffled.
Above the din the duck chimed in although his quack was muffled.

Ol' Dunny rared and broke his reins. The other horses bolted
And ran askew while feathers flew like Pegasus had molted!

I saw 'em top a distant hill a'headed home in earnest.
Like somewhere back he'd been attacked by a drunken taxidermist!

Young Orville took his chewin' square but, we finally all deduced
By Josephine, we'd never seen one ducked... instead of goosed!

And what about the duck, you ask?   Well, he didn't stay for dinner.
So I don't doubt he stuck it out,
                              or in...
                    and rode on south for winter!

THE HORSE SHOW CONVERSATION

"A fine lookin' horse you've got there *(if yer into modern art)*
I had a horse like that one time *(but he wasn't very smart)*

I'd guess that he's part thoroughbred *(and part Catahoula hound)*
You get him in a claiming race? *(or at the lost and found)*

Oh, really, you've got the papers *(I'd use'em to train the dog)*
And he's outta He's California! *(No wonder he smells like smog)*

He seems a little bit feisty *(to have one foot in the grave)*
Yup, I've used Ace myself sometimes *(when there's somethin' left to save)*

What kinda bit have you got there? *(it looks like a calving tool)*
Oh, you invented it yourself *(Do them Vise Grips make him drool?)*

Yeah, I'll bet it sure does stop him *(like runnin' into a train)*
You must of built that tie-down, too *(Never seen one made outta chain)*

And where did you get those leggin's? *(from a circus refugee)*
Well, most people like'm longer *(At least down to the knee)*

Good luck. I reckon yer up soon *(I'd hate to be in that wreck)*
You've already finished your class? *(And haven't broken yer neck)*

Two firsts and honorable mention! *(Whoa up! I'm way off the trail!)*
A fine lookin' horse you've got there *(maybe that sucker's for sale...)*

THE HORSE MUMBLER

SCENE: TWO HORSES WAITING FOR A DEMONSTRATION BY A HORSE WHISPERER.

"Hey, Ap, look who's comin'."

"It's ol' Zeb. You mean he's a horse whisperer now?"

"Well, he starved to death tryin' to rodeo, he proved it was a hard way not to make a livin'. Then he did farriery for a little while but people couldn't have their horses lame that long. Seems like he had a race horse till the track vet caught him spikin' the punch. Last I heard he was a cowboy poet."

"At least his wife had a job."

"Yeah, when he had a wife."

"So now he's a horse whisperer?"

"A horse mumbler's more like it."

"How'd he learn? Go to Equine Communication School?"

"Are you kiddin'! School! Naw, he just hung around a Ray Hunt clinic for half a day...you know he wouldn't pay to get in...and went to that movie."

"He figgered he needed a marketing gimmick. Ya know, some guys use a bullwhip or a saddle blanket or a flag. And Zeb, he wanted to be unique so he uses a big rubber bucket. His phone number is painted on the side. It's a little awkward but he's not too agile anyway so it looks natural on him."

"Look! Here he comes!"

"My gosh, what's that on his head? Looks like a Darth Vader mask with antennas!"

"Listen, he's explaining to the crowd that he has learned the language of the horse and his mask translates what he says into equine idiomatic waves that horses can understand."

"Hm, sounds like a duck to me. Uh, oh, he's getting out the bucket and heading our way!"

"Whattya reckon we should do?"

"All the local promoter said we have to do is trot around in a circle for a while, kinda act frisky, then jump in a trailer."

"What's the purpose of all this?"

"To make the equine idiotic wave operator look good."

"That's idiomatic."

"Whatever, it's not a bad day job and it sure beats workin'."

"Yeah, that's what ol' Zeb would say."

THE LIPSTICK AND THE SPUR

It's a dangerous combination . . . the lipstick and the spur.
  She had her eye on business and I had my eye on her.
It's not like you could miss her as she rode in the corral,
  The rest of us were ravaged in appearance and morale.

For six days we'd been ridin' every inch of Gilbert's place.
  The springtime wind was bitter, always hit us in the face.
The cook's camp coals were glowin' from the constant bellows wind,
  Both the steak and cherry cobbler was burnt as black as sin.

A week of never bathin' and a'cussin' every step
  Had led us to this brandin' pen, dog dirty and unkept.
But the day broke warm and sunny, we hoped not counterfeit,
  So when she rode into us, well, we all perked up a bit.

Ol' Bucker shook a loop out and he snagged a couple hooves.
  The bawlin' calf came draggin', Bucker showin' off his moves
But the flanker muffed his timing and never got a grip,
  A foot came loose and Bucker let his single dally slip.

The calf just went to floppin' like a trout out on the bank
  Then saw a little daylight underneath the horse's flank.
Ol' Bucker tossed his slack rope down to keep from gettin' hung
  But they hit the ground together, one half-hocked and one hamstrung.

Then Owen roped another calf and made it to the fire
  And sat there till the odor of a burnin' rubber tire
Assailed his tender nostrils, then he heard ol' Billy yell
  "Git out the way there, Owen, 'cause this brandin's gone to hell!"

He'd accidently roped a cow. Ol' Bill was good at that.
  She took it kinda pers'nal and became an acrobat.
His dally horn was smokin' when he let the mother go.
  She hit poor Owen's blindside, like a charging buffalo

Then Chuck, he caught a little one and put it through the fence.
  The pen filled up with ropers, competition was intense.
Don, Red, Fred, Kim and Gordie flat missed sixteen in a row
  The ground crew got to yawnin' 'cause the action was so slow.

At last a voice so gentle and so sympathetic came,
  It sounded like an angel as it quietly declaimed
"I've got a small suggestion if it's not against the code
  I can git a couple cowboys from the dairy down the road."

Then Chuck, he caught a little one and put it through the fence.
  The pen filled up with ropers, competition was intense.
Don, Red, Fred, Kim and Gordie flat missed sixteen in a row,
  The ground crew got to yawnin' 'cause the action was so slow.

The silence woke the fence posts. Every cowboy stared at her.
"Would you care to rope one, darlin'?" The boss asked, fairly sure.
She rode into the corner and she didn't wear a hat,
Her sweatshirt said *'Kiss Chris LeDoux'*, her horse was kinda fat.

She slid in nice and easy like a crafty coyote hunts
And sure as God's my witness, she roped two calves at once!
The inside leg of each one. How she did it I don't know,
Just luck, the way I see it. But it doesn't matter, though.

She took her slack and dallied, it was hard not to admire,
She jerked just once and downed 'em and drug 'em to the fire.
We waited there dumbfounded-like, the ground crew makin' hay
While the girl politely held'em like she did it every day.

We sat in handmade saddles with rawhide plaited reins
And felt the cowboy varnish a'dribblin' from our veins
But Tony summed it all up for us real buckaroos,
"Ya know, the top hand at this brandin' is wearin' tennis shoes."

There's a lesson in here somewhere about the other sex
If we could just enforce it we'd prevent a lot of wrecks.
To safeguard the equality of cowboy chromosomes
We should ask the double x's to leave their ropes at home.

THE CALF ROPER

Out of the clear blue of the Western sky
Like a dive bomber, target in the cross hairs,
Comes the cowboy equivalent of the dog fighting ace.
Tuned in like a torpedo on a string . . .
Whap-slap-two wraps and a hooey,
Faster than the human eye can see.

He was leadin' in the average 'midst the toughest competition.
    He backed up in the ropin' box and checked his ammunition,
Piggin' string, cinch tight, horn knot, rope right, horse is cocked and ready
    Thinkin' now, all clear, calf straight, right ear, hold the trigger steady,

In the box dance his caballo shimmied to the perfect spot.
    He paused a microsecond, felt the sinews coming taut,
A nod, then let the calf move, wait until you see an ear,
    Then he's on him like a cheetah runnin' down a crippled deer.

The loop sails, no, shoots... harpoon-like, through the air as thick as water.
    Horses hooves lay tracks, the cowboy leaps, it seems before he caught'er.
Down the line he slides, poppin' tucks in the jerk line, too right,
    Hand in the flank, flip and a flop, too fast to put up a fight.

The baby loop, the wrap and tie, a blur like a bullwhip crack.
    Hands in the air like a bandit whose been captured in the act.
The snappin' flag, the worried wait, the flag man rides away.
    We marvel at his wizardry, for him it's child's play.

In timed events you often hear folks ask, "Where did it go?"
    Like right before their very eyes somebody stole the show.
But ropin' calves is sleight-of-hand and magic ain't a crime,
    So all he's really guilty of is stealin' precious time.

TOM ED

Tom Ed's a good boy but missin' a screw where the clutch fits into the saw.
Everything runs but the blade never turns. Tom Ed is my brother-in-law.

I took a bad horse to the auction barn. Tom Ed came along for the ride.
That horse had a mean reputation and I figgered they'd sure skin my hide

But I got to thinkin', they're not so smart, them traders that buy everyday.
I'd teach'em a lesson once in their life, pretty soon I'd worked out a way.

"Now, listen, Tom Ed, I've got us a plan for clippin' them horse trader's wings.
You be the ringer and bid the price up. You git half, whatever he brings."

They led my ol' horse out into the ring. Tom Ed brought the bidding along.
Not bad for a kid whose table was set one salad fork short of a prong.

The auctioneer sang like a telegraph wire. Three bidders were locked in a heat
I sneaked me a peek to check out Tom Ed but Numbskull was not in his seat!

"Don't quit me, boys!" The auctioneer droned, "Now, who'll give me four twenty-five?"
Our plan was on track but just me was left to keep the bidding alive.

"Four twenty-five, a half, now a half," I nodded, "Now fifty," he said.
"Bid five, I got five, a half and now six! Just look how he carries his head!

"Seven, bid seven." I stayed in the race spurred on by the whip and the slash,
I could smell a fat hog! Dollar signs rang! I's already countin' the cash!

"Now fifty." I nodded. He bumped me up. "Eight hundred," I bid. Then I stopped.
He'd own that sucker at eight twenty-five as soon as the gavel was dropped.

"Now eight twenty-five!" The auctioneer cried, "A quarter, last chance to get on!
Ain't nobody in for eight twenty-five? Goin' once! Goin' twice!" BAM! "Goin' gone!

Sold to the bidder who just ate his hat!" I was up and huntin' Tom Ed.
He was grabbin' a bite in the cafe. He grinned, "We did it," he said,

"I started'em out then went to the john, came back just in time for the hit.
One bidder stalled but the other hung tough, I run that fool up . . . then I quit.

"Yer a genius, Bro! We sure schooled that bunch.
Them traders were sittin' ducks!
We stuck that ol' crowbait up somebody's nose
and you owe me four hundred bucks!"

FLYNT'S TRADE

Me and Flynt were tradin' horses when the thought occurred to us
We could start ourselves a business. After all, who can you trust

> If you can't trust an ol' trader who's never held a job.
> That's high praise in certain circles where the idle poor hob nob.

"We should print some stationery, buy a rabbit's foot for luck,
 Put an ad up at the sale barn, paint our motto on the truck,

> **'All things that smell like horse manure, all creatures part equinal,
> All spotted horses cost you more, of course, all sales are final.'**

We'll need to start a check account to lend ourselves repute."
I stopped Flynt's grand oration to point out we're destitute.

> "Ol' son," he sagely said to me, "We must appear successful.
> If we don't walk the rooster walk, we'll never fill our nest full."

In eight days time, our empire built, I calmly manned the phone,
Sharpened pencils, straightened horseshoes and played checkers all alone.

> No one called except Rotarians inviting us to join
> When Flynt drove up a draggin' this ol' trailer he'd purloined.

I rushed outside and helped my pard unwire the tail gate.
He was grinnin' like a twelve-year-old about to flatulate.

> "Our first big trade!," he bragged to me. "The start of our first million!"
> The horse backed out and my first thought was he looked somehow
> reptilian.

His ears had froze off near his head, his legs bowed like a lizard,
His back was humped, when he stepped out his gait severely scizzored.

> He couldn't walk a straight line true and his tail drug the ground
> So a tracker'd think a herd of kangaroos had passed through town.

His head looked like a chest of drawers, his lower lip a shovel
And from the spur tracks on his side I knew he might be trouble.

> "Got him for a song," he said, "A bargain as sure as I live."
> "So, Flynt," I said, "I'm curious, just what did you have to give?"

He turned to me, "A check," he said. His eyes went kinda funny.
"Well," said I, "I'll give you this, you sure got him worth the money."

BOB BLACK '00

133

THE MISSING LINK

It arked across the cloudless sky like someone throwin' chum
      But they weren't fishin', no my friends, the object was a thumb.
It launched from Kenneth's dally when his heelin' rope came tight
      And whizzed by Eddie's horse's head and disappeared from sight.

Eddie did a double take... hors d'oeuvres flashed through his mind,
      A little sausage on a stick that looked like Frankenstein.
"Are you okay?" He asked when Kenneth finally took a breath.
      His ropin' glove was crimson red, his face was white as death.

"Yeah, help me find my thumb," he said, "I better go, I think."
      "You go," said Ed, "I'll bring it when we've found the missing link."
The next day Eddie got a call from Kenneth's lawyer friend,
      "A suit," he said, "for negligence is what I recommend."

Well, Eddie was a bit surprised, "We packed his thumb in ice.
      We emptied out the beer and pop, a real sacrifice
And put it in the cooler then we rushed it straight on down.
      I even got a ticket speedin' comin' into town.

I've had some past experience. It's happened here before."
      "Well, we'll concede," the lawyer said, "your service was top drawer.
The packing job was excellent, but in the final sum
      In spite of all you did for Ken, you brung us the wrong thumb."

SLICK - THE SUPER HORSE

I sat on a piece of art work. It had a beating heart. A ripple ran between my legs, a tremor at the start. No more than a one on the Richter scale. A glacier calving at the limits of my sonar.

"What do I do?" I asked the artist. "Ride him," he said.

Sure. Just climb in Apollo 13 here, and take her for a spin. But I can ride, can't I? I'm supposed to be a horseman.

I tensed in the saddle. No perceptible movement, just a rush of electrical charges to my extremities in preparation. Lighter than the flutter of a fly's wing hitting a spider web. He felt it. He was instantly alert.

I clucked and shook the reins. He stepped out. Neck arched, feet placed perfectly, smooth as a glass slipper on ice. His skin shown - his mane shimmered - his stride measured - his strength apparent - his superiority unquestioned.

I became larger than life. I raised my imaginary sword. I was General Lee, King Arthur, Hernán Cortés. I was the last conquistador riding into history on a bronze horse.

A firm pressure on the throttle. An immediate response from the engine room. We kicked into a lope. I had complete confidence that he could bank, maybe even roll but I held the horizon steady.

Then laying the reins gently to his neck I signaled left. He actually turned his head back to the right and looked up at me with his big whale eye. A quick glance of irritation, a snap of impatience. "You're oversteering," said the artist, "Just the slightest touch and he'll turn. Matter of fact, just think about turning and he will."

Back into the gallop. I could hear calliope music. It is hard to ride something so majestic, so outrageous without imagining that the whole world is watching. Like escorting Lady Godiva down the aisle. You worry, 'Do I look okay? Is my hat on backwards? Will I act a fool?' But, of course no one is looking at **you**.

In my preflight check, landing instructions were simple; just say whoa. "Even running?" I asked. "Just say whoa." In the time it would take a dally to tighten, he had gone from a gallop to a dead stop. Without even touching the brakes. The depth of training to achieve this feat is profound in my mind. Just say whoa. Try that in your BMW.

How is a piece of artwork like this accomplished. Once I asked a woodcarver about a statue he'd made of a dog, "How do you do it?" He said, "I just carve away everything that doesn't look like a dog."

It strikes me that training horses is like that.

I have ridden many horses. This horse was another dimension. As true a piece of artwork as a Remington painting.

I don't know if I'll ever ride a horse that good again. It was an unexpected gift that will satisfy many longings. See, I've also never ridden in a Lamborghini . . . but now I don't have to.

DOC BAY LENA (SLICK)
owned by Roger Weibel
trained by Steve and Dori Schwartzenberger

THE ROPER'S RULE

As I look back on my career, it never did exist.
  I tried to ride the broncs and bulls, I truly did persist
But I never won a buckle. Oh, second now and then
  So now that I've got older I'm a roper, born again.
But somehow things are still the same. In fact, they've gotten worse!
  There has to be a reason why I never come in first.
Well, friends, there is. It's sad to say. I learned it yesterday.
  I was entered in a jackpot and pressin' all the way.

      McIntire was in the lead and in the final go
        His heeler single hocked their steer and dallied up real slow.
      I made a National Finals run that left the crowd in awe
        And when the dust had settled Mac and me had fought a draw!
      We gathered 'round the judge to see how he would break the tie.
        I got to wonderin' if them rules of Dress Code should apply.
      I pointed out that McIntire was wearin' tennis shoes!
        And decked out like a refugee embarking on a cruise.

Why, hell, his ratty tee shirt said, EIGHT SECONDS AIN'T SO GREAT!
  If that's no violation then there's none to violate!
The judge thumbed through his rule book to attempt to clear the fog.
  I hung onto his pant leg like a broken hearted dog.
"Oh, please pick me! I never win. There's always somethin' wrong.
  The timer's clock was faulty or the handle was too long.
My horse was old, my rope was new, the flagger was too slow.
  He ducked his head, he drug his feet. Ya listenin' Judge? Hello?

      "It's not my fault. It never is. The sun got in my eyes.
        My hat blew off, my dally slipped, I wasn't synchronized!"
      He continued to ignore me as I knelt there in the dirt.
        "You can have my stamp collection, my brand new Elvis shirt."
      I offered him my wife and kids, I'd nothing left to lose
        But he finally paid attention when I threw up on his shoes.
      He turned to McIntire and said, "He's right. You get no time."
        I skipped a beat! 'By dang,' I thought, 'I'm 'bout to hit my prime!'

After years of grim donations and payin' for the ride
  I was gonna win a buckle. It felt so good inside.
The judge looked down at me and said, "Yer gettin' second place.
  By rights that buckle should be yours but you're a special case.
The Roper's Rule applies to you. No matter how you try
  Yer doomed to be an also-ran, unlucky kind of guy.
I could ignore your conduct but I'm stickin' to my guns,
  In rodeo like real life... You whiners chafe my buns."

THE ALL RANCH RODEO

'Twas a matchup made in Elko for the cowboys in the know
  Called the Rough and Ready Knock Down Finals All Ranch Rodeo.
  Now the Texans entered up a team they thought could never lose
   When they bet their reps against the Jordan Valley buckaroos.

You could tell from where they hailed if you put 'em up for bids,
  All the buckaroos wore fancy scarves and Amish lookin' lids
   While the Texans wore their jackets for the brush down in the draws
   And them twenty dollar roll-yer-own, cheap Guatemalan straws.

It was Blucher versus Leddy, it was leggin's versus chinks
  It was rye versus tequila, it was leppies versus dinks,
   It was sagebrush versus cactus, it was ear tick versus fly,
   It was Poco Bueno versus sloggers raised on alkali.

The Texans took an early lead, at ropin' showed their stuff,
  But the buckin' horse fandango showed the buckaroos were tough.
   They branded in a dead heat, but in deference to the crowd
   Each side was harshly penalized for cussin' so dang loud.

So the teams were standin' even when the final contest came,
  UNTAMED UNGULATE EXTRACTION, wild cow milkin', by name.
   They loosed the beasts together, left their calves to bawl and mill
   And the two teams fell upon 'em like hyenas on a kill.

The buckaroo a'horseback threw his forty-footer right.
  He dallied just about the time the Texan's rope came tight.
   Their trajectories collided in a bawlin', buckin' wreck,
   The ropes and cows got tangled and they wound up neck to neck.

In the meantime two big muggers plus two others brave and bold
  Attacked the knot of thrashing hide and tried to get ahold
   Of somethin', hoof or horn or foot or spur or can of snoose.
   Then, by accident some dummy turned the bawlin' calves a'loose!

There was hair and teeth and eyeballs in the picture now and then,
  There was moustache lips and swingin' bags,
   some thought they saw a hen
    Flashin' briefly through the dust cloud. Wild images remain;
    A painting done in cow manure, a mating sandhill crane.

To describe the cataclysm would create an overload,
  But a photograph was taken and this is what it showed;
   At the summit pointed skyward were the Texas mugger's toes,
   One arm around a buckaroo, his fingers up his nose,

Who, in turn was mounted sideways splayed acrost a bally black
Who was layin' on a milker who was smashed flat on his back.
The braymer cow was balanced on her head amidst the jag,
While the Texan fought her baby for possession of the bag.

From the cyclone flew two milkers, bottles high for all to see
Like two winos at a party where the wine and cheese was free.
The buckaroo's hind leg was draggin' like he'd lost the farm.
But he kept his place by clingin' to the Texan's broken arm.

When they fell across the finish line and tumbled in the dirt
The judge declared the buckaroo the winner by a squirt.
Since the race looked pert near even, the judge said with a shrug,
"The winner is the cowboy with the most milk in his jug!"

"I object!" cried out the Texan, "Our ol' cow just had three tits!"
"That's a handicap," the judge said, "I admit it's sure the pits,
But in fairness to the buckaroo who dallys for his kicks
If you added all his fingers, he could barely count to six!"

JOHNNY WAS A MULE MAN

Johnny was a mule man, which says a lot to me.
   His motto: keep it simple. Lay it out for me to see.
   If a kid can't understand it, it's pro'bly bound to fail.
He'd rather have a good man's word than a contract in the mail.

      He never trusted horses or computers on the the shelf,
        He'd rather count the cattle, check the pasture for himself.
        If he knew you knew your business, he'd back you to the hilt
      And gladly give the credit for the fences that you built

But he'd ride you like a blanket so you couldn't go astray
   'Cause to him it all was pers'nal . . . he knew no other way.
   He didn't have the answers to each problem you were heir
But he figgered you could solve'em. That's why he put you there.

      If you could tie a diamond hitch or pour the ol' concrete
        That meant as much to him as runnin' out a balance sheet.
        See, he knew that all the business in the end came down, somehow
      To a single salaried cowboy who went out and checked a cow.

I guess he always thought himself not one of the elite
   But a man who works for wages and just got a better seat.
   And I'm sure he spent some sleepless nights doubting what he'd done
But he trusted his opinion more than almost anyone's.

      So, if he prayed, which most men do, when sleep is closing in,
        He pro'bly prayed that Scottish prayer that suited men like him,
        "Lord, grant that I am right, that my judgement's not gone blind.
      For Thou knowest in Thy wisdom, it's hard to change my mind."

DIED AND COME BACK TO LIFE

Have you heard of those folks who claim to have died
  And then have come back to life?
  They speak of a glimpse of a heavenly place
Far from the world and its strife.

    The stories they tell have a common thread.
     To a man they all contend
     They found themselves in a long dark tunnel
    With a light at the other end.

Now as you might surmise there are skeptics
  That think it's mostly hot air
  But I can confirm they're not blowin' smoke
'Cause friends, I know . . . I was there.

    I was entered up in the fall rodeo
     And drawed a bull named Big Red.
     Just when I had him . . . he bucked me clean off!
    I lit right square on my head.

I hit the ground like a bag of loose salt.
  Knocked me plum out, so they said.
  Little stars twinkled around in my brain,
For all I knew I was dead.

    I righted myself, or thought I was righted,
     I might have been upside down
     But, there I was in that long dark tunnel.
    I marveled at what I found,

'Cause down at the end just like they had said
  A light materialized.
  I squinted my eyeballs and studied that light,
It was then I realized

    My collar encircled my head like a wreath?
     At last it finally made sense,
     I was peekin' out through a button hole . . .
    So I crawled back up on the fence.

TWO JUMPS

Two Jumps said he used to ride bulls. In spite of his name, he tried.
He had grit, determination and bravado on his side.

Unfortunately, he lacked skill. He was naturally inept
and as life laid down her cowpies, that's precisely where he stepped.

But even a hard luck cowboy's entitled to one guru
whose faith in him is undaunted, whose loyalty stays true blue.

Now, all of the young bronc stompers and bullriders knew Lecile.
A rodeo clown and hero to all who strapped on the steel.

Lecile knew the bulls and broncs and always offered advice
on rodeo, on love and life, on learnin' to sacrifice.

It was over the chutes at Knoxville when Two Jumps heard the phrase
that would stay with him forever, long after those heady days.

Lecile was walkin' toward him, no doubt, to wish him well.
Two Jumps cut eyes at his pardners to make sure they all could tell

It was him Lecile had chosen to pass along for this ride
the words he was meant to live by. He fairly bursted with pride.

Two Jumps was pullin' his bullrope, the rosin startin' to smoke
when Lecile looked over the chute gate, squinted his eyes, then he spoke,

"Two Jumps," Lecile confided, ***"To really make yourself proud,
ain't no way you can ride this bull... so hang up and thrill the crowd!"***

SALESMAN'S DILEMMA

I had sold a magic bolus to a farmer.
     It was guaranteed to rid his herd of flies
It would pass out with the pucky
     and if everyone got lucky
It would kill the eggs the flies laid in the pies.

     He had bought enough to do a hundred critters.
          "These had better work," he said, "They cost enough."
     "I can guarantee they'll do it,
          I'll come out and take you through it,
     You just follow the directions for the stuff."

I drove out and found the farmer nearly finished
     But the scene I saw sent shivers up my spine
Was the A.I. tech invited?
     Had the farmer grown near sighted?
'Cause a crowd was gathered 'round the cow's behind.

     In the middle wearin' goggles and a slicker
          Smeared with green effluent like he'd hit the fan,
     Dressed in pre-composted splendor,
          Poised at ready to rear-end her,
     Stood the farmer with a balling gun in hand.

"How's it goin', boys," I asked with trepidation.
     "Well, this bothers some cows more than I'd 'uve thought.
This procedure don't impress her."
     I said, "Try a tongue depressor."
But I knew that all his work had been for naught.

     So I watched him put the bolus,...I can't say it.
          My commission check was goin' up in smoke.
     I was gonna take a skinnin'
          Then the whole crew started grinnin'
     And I realized they'd staged it as a joke!

At the office when I told my boss the story
     He got livid, said I'd bolluxed up the sale,
"Now we'll have to go redo'em,
     What the heck did you say to'em?"
"Well, since they only had ten left... I held the tail."

147

PESTILENCE

Piojos! Lice! The biting kind. You see'em everywhere!
They're thick as thieves on cattle's backs and crawlin' in their hair!

And ticks the size of Tootsie Pops transfuse a cow a day!
And two can pack a yearlin' off or pull a one-horse sleigh!

A team of scabies mites can slick a pen of weaners clean
And make you wish you'd never heard of two-dip quarantine!

But sheep don't get off easier, there's nasal bots and keds
Plus maggots from a screwworm strike that every herder dreads.

There's deer flies, blow flies, horn flies, house, face flies, horse flies, warbles.
There's pinworms, hookworms, lungworms, tapes. Nasty, horrid, horribles!

As if them buggers ain't enough, row croppin' can be worse!
It's hard to make a cotton crop if bollworms get there first!

And if you think I'm blowin' smoke try growin' grapes or pears
When aphids, thrips and nematodes all take their rightful shares.

They took ol' Noah at his word, "Go forth and multiply!"
But man has stepped into the breach and raised the battle cry!

We're fighting back with pesticides, with dips and sprays and dust.
With tags and bags and fogging guns, "Insecticides or Bust!"

We applicate them airily, we mix it from a sack,
We give it in a shot nowdays or pour it down their back.

We hire consultants left and right to give us sound advice
So we can fight this pestilence of worms and flies and lice.

We tell ourselves God gave us brains to halt their ill effect
And, though He made all living things He gave us intellect.

So, how come we can't beat these bugs? Methinks we've too much pride.
Though God made us, remember He ain't always on our side!

148

SHE DOES THE BOOKS

This is my wife. She does the books.
  I do the important stuff
Like mend the fence and check the cows,
  She makes sure the income's enough

To cover the cost of farmin'.
  She's tight as a new hat band.
I need to buy a new baler,
  She figgers out if we can.

I spend all day in the pickup,
  She's in the office all day
Just talkin' with the SCS
  Or checkin' the price of hay

Or dealin' with the accountants
  And keepin' the banker straight.
I might be cleanin' a ditch out
  Or hangin' a rusty gate.

She fills out all the blasted forms
  The government makes us keep.
She reads those regulations till
  She's fightin'em in her sleep.

Me, I go to sleep a'dreamin'
  Of bulls and barns and sales,
She's dreamin' the inventory
  Or estimatin' bales.

She still finds time to bake a pie
  Between her business deals
And I keep busy all the time
  Just greasin' squeaky wheels.

I told my wife that we should think
  'Bout gettin' a hired man.
Runnin' a place ain't easy,
  Good managers need a plan.

She agreed that it weren't easy
  To manage and keep abreast
"But, why," she asked, "Get a hired man?
I've already got the best."

151

THE COWBOY BRIDE

All the usual suspects were lined up behind the groom.
The smell of cheap tequila rose from their side of the room.
They looked like boneless chickens, plucked and feelin' none too good,
All the victims of the night before's farewell to bachelorhood.

The bride was making mental notes to have the best man flogged,
To doublecheck the ladies room that earlier had clogged,
Regretting that the rented tuxes weren't a better fit
And hoping that the photographs would not show up her zit.

The preacher opened up his Book and beamed a practiced smile,
"We are gathered here together....get that kid out of the aisle!
He's standing on your train and leaving chocolate finger marks!"
She turned and hissed, "Git off my dress or I'll feed you to the sharks!"

The kid jumped off the wrinkled train - but sister filled the gap
She grabbed the end and gave it one good *change the sheets* type snap.
The whole thing came off in her hands! The bride, once fully dressed,
From thong to slippers now was bared to the assembled guests.

Just then the bridesmaid groaned and ran back toward the potted plants.
The bug-eyed preacher stopped and stared, then cast his eyes askance.
"It's morning sickness," said the bride, "She's gonna have to blow.
I've got it, too," she whispered, "So just get on with the show."

"The ring?" The preacher asked the groom. But he was in a trance.
The best man nudged him gently, then reached down in his pants,
"My pocket's got a hole in it! The ring's gone down to my boot!"
"Well, get it out!" the bride replied, "I'm not too proud to shoot."

In stocking foot the best man helped the groom present the ring.
The bridesmaid in her spotted dress stood by encouraging.
But when they went to place the ring upon the groom's left hand,
He keeled over backwards knocking out the poor best man.

The new bride caught the preacher's eye...Impaled him with a glare,
"He does," she said, "And so do I." Her challenge filled the air.
"Then I pronounce you man and wife...Let nothing gang aglay.
I wish you all the very best....you may drag the groom away."

Some might think this cowboy marriage was ordained an early death.
But friends, if you had seen her....not as long as she drew breath.
She just threw him in the pickup, popped the clutch and waved goodbye
With the dog up front beside her, lookin' life right in the eye.

153

FIRST DANCE

I danced with another woman tonight.
       My wife didn't seem to mind.
    We took to the floor like a pair of swans
       that fate forever entwined.

      Leaving our wake through the dancers who flowed
         Like notes in search of a song
      We tested our two step, tried out a waltz
        and laughed when something went wrong!

I led and she followed, trusting each step,
      spurred by the beat of the band
Like birds taking wing the very first time,
      it helps to hold someone's hand.

      Although I had known this woman before
        I'd thought of her as a child
      But there on the dance floor, arm 'round her waist,
        I found my heart was beguiled.

For her a window had opened. I was there,
      I'm eternally glad.
The rest of my life I'll remember
      the first night
          she danced with her dad.

A FATHER'S THOUGHTS AT GRADUATION

Did you ever stop and think to yourself, 'This will be the last time...'

Well, today will be the last time I'll kiss my little girl. Tomorrow she steps into womanhood. Confident, confused, comely, coltish, curious, charming, garrulous, fierce and fearing.

Who will take care of her. Who will she love. What will she remember. What will she forget. What star will guide her.

Will she forgive herself when she can't always live up to her own expectations. Will she choose the right way when the easy path beckons.

Will she discover the difference between pride and vanity, between courage and posing, between distance and privacy.

Will she experience the joy of the golden rule, the heartbreak of losing, the satisfaction of an anonymous kindness, the love of a child.

Will the boulders in her life make her strong or break her spirit.

How will she handle random acts of fate, accidents and blessings. Will she need to assign blame.

Will she make messes or clean them up.

Will she find passion in her life, of the mind and heart. A burning, a yearning, a calling, a cause, a reason to get up every day.

Will she know peace of mind, contentment, solace in her own company.

Will life be good to her.

And will she always know that no matter what happens, I will always love her. That she will carry the burden of my love even when we are separated by miles and years and harsh words and the vacuum of minutiae, even beyond life itself.

So many questions.

So, today I stand here, quietly thinking all these thoughts as I watch her whirl about in preoccupied flurry, knowing this will be the last time... She will be a woman in the blink of an eye.

And as I kiss her cheek, I can only ask, "Where did she go, this little girl of mine."

DUROC OR CHARDONEY

The pork producers are to be commended. They have worked long and hard to improve the image of pork. For centuries pigs and fat have been connected at the jowl.

Porky, piggish, pig pen, pig-headed, pig-eyed, hoggish, ham handed, hamstrung, pork barrel, hog wash, sow's ear, boar's nest, pig sty and pig in a poke are all terms that have become common when wishing to insult some human's appearance or behavior. I've always admired those resolute loyal women who wore the banner proclaiming them Pork Princess.

But when the farmers changed the product (the market hog himself), they changed the public's perception of pork as well. I thought *The Other White Meat* advertising slogan - a clever tie-in with chicken - was imaginative. I'm amazed how well it has sunk into the consumer's brain. 'Course when they named it that, I don't think the pork producers ever figured it would be the same price!

But be that as it may, I've been plotting their next piggy back advertising relationship. One that will move them into a new level of sophistication and acceptance. How does this sound, "We shall serve no swine before its time."

"That's right friends, National Hog Farms can become the Ernest and Julio Gallo of pork. Imagine two obviously happy, environmentally conscious, grandfather types appearing on the television each holding a smoked ham singing the praises of pork. We'd see billboards with thirty somethings on a beach somewhere smiling and toasting each other with a cracklin'.

North Carolina would become the Napa Valley of the pig business. People would plan vacations to swine country. They could go by the individual swineries for samples of head cheese, pickled pigs feet, Baco bits, and sausage. On college campuses faculty would engage in swine and cheese parties.

Swine tasting would become an art form. At restaurants the Hamnelier (swine server) would bring out your entree, cut your first bite using special tongs and a pig sticker (sorry) and proffer it to your lips. You would sniff, suck, masticate, savor and swallow. "Excellent, Hervé. It has a certain candor, a frankness that says 'I'm from Oklahoma and proud of it.' Haughty, but not coy, a boldness reminiscent of Javelina '55. Yet juicy and succulent, stepping into the new millennium while keeping a cloven appendage firmly ensconced in . . . "

"OH SHUT UP!"

Forgive me, I got carried away. But it's not often I can see this clearly into the future. Pop the Cork on Pork!

THE TOAST

It gives me great pleasure to stand here today
to heap limelight on one in our midst
Who has mastered the art of vulgar display yet,
when asked to desist it . . . he didst
There are those among us who are more qualified
to encouch in a language precise
The discrepant reasons of why you abide
with us always, like typhus or lice
Why I have been chosen, I cannot explain I've no keen repartee to impart
But I'm honored, so, though my words may seem plain be assured that
they come from the heart . . .

You mare ridin', mouth breathin', egg suckin' skunk
Yer the kind who drowns kittens for fun
You hat stealin', hole peepin', pencil neck punk
Yer a blister on everyone's bun

You dog kickin', mule whippin', carp eatin' crud
Yer a bagful of grizzly bear bait
You never sweat, no workin', blank shootin' dud
Yer the reason for bicarbonate

You lackluster, festering, double dumb putz
Yer the wax on a tom turkey's snood
You buzzard breath, bone pickin', big tub of guts
Yer a flake of the first magnitude

You scrofulous, wool slippin', miscreant scum
Yer the grease off a Hell's Angles' comb
You bilgewater, bog drinkin', boot lickin' bum
Yer a bucket of thundermug foam

You counterfeit, card cheatin', common bred clump
Yer the fungus in old cottage cheese
You back stabbin', beady eyed, Bactrian hump
Yer a throwback to when we climbed trees

To sum up yer good points could be quite a chore there's so many that
it's hard to say
You're either au jus off a dog kennel floor or the nit in a wino's toupee
Regardless, we love ya. I don't like to boast but our standards are really
quite high
And though you seem lacking, I'll offer a toast 'cause the truth is,
yer our kinda guy!

THE CAT LIKED POPCORN

The cat liked popcorn.

It could have been a Christmas story but it wasn't. It was young Ty's eighth birthday. He had his heart set on a baby hamster. Kim was a Boon & Crockett mother and set out to fill her young cub's needs.

The night of Birthday Eve she camouflaged a trip to the pet store as a movie with Ty's big brother. At the pet store she excitedly told the salesman of the great hamster surprise. The pet store person warned her against leaving the baby hamster, no bigger than an avocado pit, in the cardboard box in the car. "It'll eat right through that cardboard like white hot magma through a styrofoam cup. Then it will shred the front seat of your car and make an upholstery bed big as a condor's nest. Best keep it close!"

Kim went into the theater with baby hamster in her jacket pocket. By the end of the previews the wiley rodent had gnawed through the pocket and was thrashing his way through the lining. The movie began with an ear shattering clap of thunder and built from there. With every blood curdling scream, structure dropping explosion and metal tearing collision, the baby hamster fought and clawed his confining cloth bonds!

He spent the last half of the movie rolled up in mama lion's shirt front drawing blood on a regular basis.

She made it home, woke Ty up and unceremoniously presented him with his birthday hamster. Popcorn, so named because of his introduction to the movies, spent the night in the bathtub.

The light of day diminished the anguish of the night before for mom. She helped Ty construct the elaborate hamster cage complete with tubes, automatic waterer, ferris wheels, bumper cars and the non-chewable, inescapable, indestructible maximum security hamster haven. It cost $30.

The family went to town that evening for Ty's birthday dinner. Giddy and satisfied with cake and candles they returned home to find the cat polishing off it's own birthday dinner. A little stump of a tail that stuck out of his mouth was still showing between cheeks full of hamster hams.

There was not much anyone could do except note the unlatched cage door, so they left the cat to finish his meal.

Ty was distraught and developed pinkeye, Strep throat, an ear infection, sinus and began walking with a limp. However he did achieve a complete recovery before the last of the rodent bites healed on mama's finger.

159

VISITING DOGS

When I hear a truck pull up in front of the house and the pandemonium of dogs barkin' that would wake a hibernating mastodon, I relax. It's only my neighbor, D. K., come to borrow something of his back.

He doesn't get this ferocious reception because he's on the canine list of unsavory visitors or because he has the reputation of annoying domestic animals on a regular basis. It's because his two dogs usually accompany him on his rounds.

My dogs even bark at his pickup when he drives in anticipating that his dogs will be in the back. On those rare occasions when he comes "undogged", my dogs give him a withering glare and stomp off. It's like they are disappointed.

After all, what else have they got to do? Watch the sheep through the fence? Go to the pasture and check the cows. Sneak up on the creek in hopes of scaring the urea out of the ducks.

I watched them the last time I went to D. K.'s to borrow his brush hog. My dogs were leaning out the side already clearing their throats as we neared his place. I deliberately drove by the first turn-in. Both dogs jerked their heads around and glared at me through the back window. I could see Hattie mouthing the words, "Hey turkey, ya missed it!"

I turned in the second drive and we were met with the raucous sounds of a rabbit let go in a dog kennel. I pulled to a stop as D. K.'s dogs surrounded the pickup barking at the top of their dog lungs.

My dogs were leaning out over the side like seasick fishermen returning in kind, bark for bark. It was deafening.

But I noticed D. K.'s dogs never got quite close enough to touch noses and mine knew just how far to lean to avoid actual contact.

One might think it was all for show. Protecting their territory, as if his were shouting, "Don't you dare get out", and mine were screaming, "No way we're lettin' you jump in this truck!"

Or they could just be visiting like old folks at a reunion, "HOW ARE YOU, TEX! I HEAR YOU GOT A NEW HEARING AID! WHAT KIND IS IT?"

"QUARTER TO FOUR!"

I've gotten to where I don't worry about it much. Dogs like to bark. It's in their job description. It probably doesn't irritate the dogs near as much as it does us humans. They just communicate at different decibel levels. It's part of nature. It's possible even aphids bark at each other and we just can't hear it. But it must drive the ants crazy.

160

RC AND BUD

R.C. is an animal lover. Maybe not the kind of animal lover that the term has come to mean in this era of animal rights activism, but the kind that requires a greater commitment.

He would tell you he's a farmer. But he's a horseman and trainer, cattleman, hog producer, corn grower and great-grandfather. He's also a dog man, with the patience and persistence to deserve a good stock dog.

R.C. has had a wide variety of dogs in his life. One day he asked his wife, Doris to keep an eye out for a Blue Heeler. They appealed to him but he'd never had one. 'Kinda rough dogs.' he thought.

Soon she found one advertised in the Albia paper; a two year old male lookin' for a home. R.C. was suspicious. Takin' on a dog that old was risky. Bad habits would be developed, old loyalties established. One just never knew.

"Well, it wouldn't hurt to look," Doris chided him.

Finally, three weeks later R.C. went by to look at the dog. As Doris was introducing themselves to the lady of the house, the two year old blue merle walked right up to R.C. and looked at him. They exchanged studious looks - something unspoken passed between them. R.C. picked the dog up under his arm and took him to the truck.

He just knew. The way some people know when a guitar string is in tune or a steak is cooked just right. R.C. knew the dog would be fine. And, I think the dog must have come to the same conclusion because they became constant outdoor companions. He named him Bud.

162

Two months after Bud had moved in with them, R.C. was out feeding. He slung a bushel basket of ear corn over his shoulder and walked into the pig pen. Bud was dawdling by the gate.

Sixteen sows came squealing from the corner as R.C. approached. His foot hit something. He slipped, went down on his back, cracked his head on a rock, and was knocked unconscious.

His last memory as he fell was a three ton wall of hungry sows charging.

He woke to find himself looking skyward in the pig pen with sticky blood on his face, in his hair and on his shirt. Bud had worn a circle around his sprawled out body. Just a few feet away the sows waited, watching, a dark look in their eyes. Several ears of corn still lay by his head. Bud stood guard.

Another true dog story like we hear so often. If R.C. had not been an animal lover, would it have had a different ending?

But from their first meeting, dog and man somehow sensed that they would be there for each other. I can't explain how it works, it's beyond me. But it wasn't beyond Bud . . . he just knew.

~~BAXTER~~ ~~BLACK~~

ON THE EDGE OF COMMON SENSE

by Bailey

Der frendz and felo cowdogz. It wuz Thanx gibing. Not to xiting. Mabe I wuz hopping for to much.

A teem roppin, sum bunge jumping, a baryd pig. Yoo no, sumthing with zubstanshul bonz. But no, only terke.

Cors, OnkL Gim sluuzed aduzen kwaL from the royo whish tha barbkwood down to the ziz of OnkL Gimz thum. Tha skotrd uz a fu kwaL leftofers with. Lik eting mach stiks with bukshot inum. I felt an auL.

Thar wuz lotz of kids wich me an Haty Lik. Speshale the LidL wons. Tha R olwaz drappin fud or if the gron upz R bize, a clevr dog kan ujate Likit rit of thar plat or fas.

Bakster the grat az he cals himself, wuz trin to bee the hozt. I saw him carf the terky. Sumhow he wownd up with thre drumstix, haf a wesh bon, a standing rib rost, thre powns of samuh ro and a chjkn nek! No wunder tha made him kwit vetanary surjure.

Kupl haba leenas wunderd bi. Tha got to cloz to the horzechu gam. Won of OnkL Gimz throz got awa an nerle unikd the por bugr.

Didnt take much to skarum awa. Not like the buzrdz. The ski was blak withum! Musta bin Bumbling Bakstrs smokt helk sosag.

Evrebud lad arond lik hienuz aftur a bufalo zuersid. Ever cee a pithon aftur hes swaLoy a tapir?

I admit I wuz stuff miself. But I fownd the kwaLgutz wich helpt mi dijechun. kinda kep the ol inurdz churnin an bub Lin. It was powrful to B arown! cors tha al blamd OnkL Gim an Baketr.

servsum rit.

Hapy Thanxgibin yaL. yer fren BaiLy

JUST A DOG

You were just a dog. But a good dog.

Right from the start. Your loyalty was never in question. And what you didn't know, you didn't know because I never took the time to teach you.

When you were young I was harder on you. I expected you to understand the basics... and you learned them. A *"bad dog"* was like a whip on your back.

But when uncontrollable instinct got you in trouble, I didn't hold it against you. I doctored you up, changed your bed and remembered that reason gets left behind in the heat of passion. Be it skunks, gyps or cloven hooves.

You were patient with the young, pups or kids. They pulled your hair, barked around you in circles and rode on your back. I never had to worry. They were safe with you.

You suffered the indignities of veterinary examinations, injections, probings and overnight incarcerations, refusing always to lift your leg under *anyone's* roof.

You posed for pictures, rode on loads like an acrobat and endured spring clippings yet never lost your sense of dignity.

A fierce guardian of your territory, you did your best to protect us. I knew better than to shout you down at two in the morning. I always figgered you were barking for a purpose.

Old age was not unkind to you. Despite the hearing loss, cataracts and stiff joints, you carried on. Sure, I had to help you get in the pickup, but you were part of the crew. I noticed you ate less, slept late and turned gray but you never lost your enthusiasm for bein' part of our outfit.

People debate if dogs have a heaven. I'm not sure that matters. What is heaven to a dog? Enough to eat, something to chase, shade in the summer, someone to scratch your ears and pay you a little attention now and then.

All I know is you added to our life. Companion, listener, guardian and connection to a part of nature we tend to overlook because we're too busy worrying about the minutia of life.

You reminded us to appreciate a sunny day, a bone to chew and a kind word. You'll be missed around here.

You were just a dog. But you'll be in my heaven. Rest in peace, old friend.

THE BORDER COLLIE SOLILOQUY

Just a word about one of the greatest genetic creations on the face of this earth . . . the border collie.

Faster than a speeding bullet. More powerful than a locomotive. Able to leap tall fences in a single bound.

The dog that all sheep talk about but never want to meet. The fur that legends are made of. Makes coyotes cringe, sheep trip the light fantastic and eagles soar somewhere else.

Invested with the energy of a litter of puppies, the work ethic of a boat person and the loyalty of Lassie, they ply their trade on sagebrush flats, grassy fields and precipitous peaks from sea to shining sea.

"Away to me!" I command. They streak and sail, zipping like pucks on the ice. Black and white hummingbirds, in out, up down, come by.

Sheep. With head up, one eye cocked over their shoulder asking directions. To the gate through the race. Mighty dog moves behind the bunch like a towboat pushing barges around a bend.

And heart. Do they try? "Just let me at'em, Dad!" Stay! "C'mon, I'm ready!" Stay! "Can't you feel me hummin'? Listen to my heart, it's purrin' like a cat! I am primed! Aim me, point me, pull the trigger!"

"Away to me!" It makes me feel like Robin Hood. He leaves my side like an arrow.

Workin' dogs is like manipulating a screwdriver with chopsticks. Like doing calligraphy with a plastic whip. Like bobbing for apples. Like threading a needle with no hands. Like playing pool on the kitchen table.

There are no straight lines in nature. Only arcs. Great sweeping curves of sight and thought and voice and dog. Always having to lead your command about a dog's length.

Sheep bunched like logs on the river. Dogs paddling in the current, always pushing upstream. A ewe breaks loose. Then another. Another. The log jam breaks. Dogs and sheep tumble about in the white water.

Calm again, they start back upstream.

Border collies. Are they truly smarter than a chimpanzee? Cuddlier than a koala? More dedicated than Batman's valet?

Can they change course in mid air? Drag Nell from the tracks and locate the missing microfilm?

Yes. I believe they can. They are the best of the best, the epitome of 'above and beyond the call of duty'. Head Dog. Top Gun.

I salute you, for man has never had a better friend.

THE DOG AND THE RABBIT

Have you ever been embarrassed by yer good dog? Me either! I've got a good dog. An Australian shepherd with one blue eye and I believe he loves me. I believe I love him. He'll go with me anywhere. When I say, "You wanna go?" He don't ask, "Where you goin'? Goin' by the video store?" No, he don't care, he just wants to go. And did you ever notice that it don't matter whether you been gone five minutes or five days, yer dog is so glad to see ya. Can you think of a single human that is that glad to see ya? Yer fixin' to leave, walk out to the pickup and forget somethin' so you run back inside. Yer dog licks yer hand. Your spouse says, "I thought you left!"

I've got a neighbor. A good neighbor. And when you live on the outskirts a good neighbor is someone who lives just the right distance away. Close enough to circle the wagons but far enough away to allow that privacy people like us seem to value, *("I believe those are Texas plates, Mother," he said, sighting through his binoculars)*.

Anyway, my neighbor gets home 'bout a quarter after five every day. She goes through the house and comes out the back door wearin' her cover-alls. In her backyard she has a long line of rabbit hutches and she spends, what is to me, an inordinate amount of time messin' with them rabbits . . . talkin' to 'em . . . singin' 'em little rabbit songs.

Now I'm sittin' out on the back porch one afternoon in my porch swing. It's about 2:30. I'm done workin'. I've already thought up somethin'. I look out in the driveway and there's my good dog and he has got . . . and you know how you can tell from a distance it ain't a jackrabbit? They aren't black and white, they don't have them big floppy ears, and he has got this rabbit between his teeth and he's thrashin' him like a shark with a ham hock! There's dirt and leaves and brush and gravel flyin' all over. I jump up and grab that rabbit! "Go git in the pickup you... *#@^. . .!" That rabbit looked bad. Looked like he caught on fire and somebody put him out with the weedeater!

I ran in the house and run the tub full of warm water. Tested it with my elbow. Then I got some of my wife's good shampoo. She gets it at Holiday Inn, it ain't that big a deal. I sudsed him up twice then moused him with my daughter's mousse. Made him sticky. You could thwack him on the tile, peel him off like Velcro. Then I run upstairs to the laundry and put him in the dryer. When he came out he was fluffy, looked like an electrocuted porcupine!

I carried him to my neighbor's house. Sure enuf the last hutch on the end was cocked open and it was empty. I took that rabbit and folded him . . into a rabbit position. Put a smile on his lips, all three of 'em. Gave him a chew of Red Man and leaned him up against the wire.

I went back to the house and commenced to rockin'. 'Bout a quarter after five I saw my neighbor drive up, she got out, went through the house and came out the back wearin' her covies. She started down that long line of rabbit hutches. Talkin' to 'em. Singin' 'em little rabbit songs. "Here comes Peter Cottontail, hoppin' down the bunny trail..." All of a sudden I heard her scream!

I ran over there, bein' the good neighbor that I was, "What's wrong? What's wrong?"

"My rabbit," she cried.

I looked in the cage and the poor little duffer had fell over. One ear broke off. It didn't look good.

I stroked him gently and said, "Ma'am, I b'lieve he is dead."

I was a veterinarian, I could tell that.

"Yes," she said, "But what bothers me is I buried him three days ago!"

LIFE IS A COMPROMISE

They tell me Wally is smokin' again,
But life is a compromise.
He's tried to kill himself so many ways,
The heart was not a surprise.

I guess he's lucky they found him in time.
Was close, as I understand.
Pickups on dirt roads at breakneck speed,
Would'a killed a lesser man.

The nurses said he was pleasant at times . . .
When he was anesthetized.
But alas, he relapsed back to normal,
His arteries revulcanized.

It was awful to watch his recovery,
His forced marches down by the wood.
Striding along in his tennies and
He's quit eating everything good.

Begrudgingly he's gettin' better,
Got horseback, but some things have changed.
He's growin' a beard and he's writing
His memoirs out on the range.

He's givin' the kids a little more slack,
At runnin' the home ranch outfit.
Of course, they threatened to leave him next time,
If he didn't back off a bit.

So he's still the biggest buck in the herd
And goes around leavin' his scrape,
And buglin' some. . . But he's careful now
'Bout who he gets bent outta shape.

So, the fact I hear that he's smokin' again
Is sort of what I would expect.
With his rebuilt heart he's prob'ly deduced
There's not much left to protect.

I asked if his doctors agreed with his scheme
He said, "Nope, their warnings were stern,
Said sooner or later they'd see him again . . .
But they wouldn't be near as concerned."

REINDEER FLU

You remember that Christmas a few years ago
    When you waited all night for ol' Santy to show
        Well, I heard the reason and it just might be true
    The whole bunch came down with the dang reindeer flu

The cowboy elves had been busy all day
    A doctorin' Donner and scatterin' hay
        Dancer and Prancer were febrile and snotty
    Comet and Cupid went constantly potty

Hallucinatory dementia was rampant
    Why, Blitzen imagined that he was Jed Clampett
        Dasher got schizo and thought he was Trigger
    While Vixen's obsessions got bigger and bigger

By noon Santy knew they should find substitutes
    So the cowboy elves went out searching recruits
        They scoured the Arctic for suitable prey
    And brought them together to hook to the sleigh

When Santy climbed up it was like a bad dream
    He stared down the lines at the substitute team
        A bull moose as old as the planks on the Ark
    With a head as big as a hammerhead shark

Stood hitched by a cow, Mrs. Santy's of course
    Then next in the tugs was a Clydesdale horse
        He was paired with an elk whose antlers were crossed
    An ostrich, a walrus, an old albatross

Were harnessed in line but the last volunteer
    Was a blue heeler dog with only one ear
        The cowboy elves gave a push to the sled
    As Santy rared back, cracked his whip, then he said

"On Cleo, on Leo, on Lefty and Jake,
    On Morphus, Redondo, On Lupe and Snake . . ."
        Smoke from the runners cut tracks in the snow
    The team headed south, but, where else could they go.

They started back East 'cause it got dark there first
    And their luck, which was bad, got progressively worse
        By the time they hit Kansas the tugs had gone slack
    And all but the dog was now ridin' in back

Santy was desperate. What on earth could he do?
　　　Then the lights of an airport hove into his view
　　　　　Did they make it? You betcha, but here hangs the tale
　　　Of how, on that Christmas they stayed on the trail

A man in Alaska said right after dawn
　　　A low flying object passed over his lawn
　　　　　He ran to the window and threw up the sash
　　　And heard someone shouting, "Fer Pete's sake, don't crash!

On Budget, On Thrifty, look out Alamo
　　　I didn't take out the insurance, you know
　　　　　And you, Number Two, try harder, yer Avis
　　　On Dollar, On Hertz, Rent-a-Wreck, you can save us

An extra day's charge if we make it by nine
　　　Though the drop off will cost us a bundle this time
　　　　　Merry Christmas," yelled Santy, but he was all smiles
　　　'Cause at least he'd signed up for unlimited miles

So that's how it happened as best I recall
　　　When it looked like that Christmas might not come at all
　　　　　And the truth of the matter, we all owe a cheer
　　　To the Wichita office of Rent-a-Reindeer

CHRISTMAS OFFICE PARTY IN THE BARNYARD

At the Christmas office party in the barnyard on the farm,
The domesticated Dilberts were dispensing wit and charm.
The fermented grain made scholars out of even dullest fowl,
Though it's hard to take a chicken seriously, even when he's speaking owl.

Sheep were bunched like secretaries, sipping wine, comparing notes,
'bout the latest in-house romance and, like always, blamed the goats.
While the sheep dog and the llama were discussing coyotehood,
and why they liked the N.R.A. and would belong if animals could,
And why it's so misunderstood.

Cows were gathered round the milk bowl with the union Galloway
Who was trying to convince them they should strike for higher hay.
The more they drank the more they plotted out their smartest moves,
But they finally gave the plan up 'cause its hard to hold a picket sign,
If all you've got is cloven hooves.

By then the pigs had made a mess of all the hors d'oeuvre trays,
"We're unappreciated swine - You think we live our days
Just eat and drink and wallow but WE have yearnings, too!
We aspire to upper management, maybe even Vice President in charge of
rooting," (it was mostly moonshine talkin') Put a pig in sales now!
It was all this discontentment that had got them feelin' blue.

Farmer Brown announced the bonus like he did most every year.
They could all take Christmas Day off which was greeted with a cheer.
They had tried to guess the bonus, but like always they could not,
Everytime they were astounded and surprised which some might think
was silly because it was the same thing every Christmas,
But, like always, they forgot,

As the sun set on the barnyard everybody got depressed,
Just another office party that would fade into the rest.
Till the rooster's inspiration saved this ponderous December,
When he caught the big tom turkey weaving slightly underneath the
mistletoe, mistook him for a piñata and nearly took his head off with a
fence stay, causing a small laceration of the snood but as memories will
attest, made this a Christmas to remember.

175

SANTY'S EMISSION STICKER

The word came down last Christmas that Santy was not in compliance.
    His mode of transportation fell far short of the standards of science.
The E.P.A. and D.O.T. proclaimed, and here's the real kicker,
    He'd be required to now possess an official emissions sticker.

So off he went to Fort McMurray, the nearest inspection station.
    He drove his team in through the door and was met by a congregation
Of worker ants and clipboard kings all looking so officious.
    "Connect the hoses!" the head man said. The reindeer got suspicious.

"And be aware of pressure leaks, those backfires can be brutal.
    Now rev the RPMs up high and we'll check the whole caboodle."
The carbon dioxide blinking lights began illuminating.
    "A direct result," the inspector said, "of reindeer ruminating."

"The methane levels must be checked out to protect from global warming."
    "Relax," said Santy, "the after burners will keep the methane conforming."
"Just one more test," the inspector said, "to check for particulate matter."
    He kicked the RPMs on up. All thirty-two hooves made a clatter.

"You better back off," Santy shouted... but too late. The tragic result;
    The hoses blew and the reindeer flew like jets off a catapult!
The blast blew out all the windows, eclipsed the A. Borealis.
    Lit up the Kremlin in Moscow and darkened the streets of Dallas.

It knocked the moon outta orbit and started an Arctic tsunami.
    It broke up a mortician party, just when it was gettin' embalmy.
A mushroom cloud arose from the scene, a silent but deadly convector,
    Below, knee deep in emissions stood the intrepid inspector.

He gathered up his dignity with a minimum of swearin'.
    Then with the edge of his clipboard and the hard hat he'd been wearin',
He collected the solid particulates to complete ol' Santy's packet
    By scrapin' the requisite samples off the front of his jacket.

WHAT'S CHRISTMAS TO A COW?

I know you've prob'ly asked yourself, what's Christmas to a cow?
You've not! Well maybe, just perchance I've got you thinkin' now,
When we march out on Christmas morn like nothin's goin' on,
Has Yuletide struck the night before and disappeared by dawn?
Were plastic sleeves a'hangin' up around the calvin' shed?
Did visions of molasses blocks cavort inside her head?
And did she lay awake all night tensed up anticipating
Or, in excitement, milk her bed by accident, while waiting?
Do cows pretend to be just cows, devoid of all intrigues
But really lead a secret life like women's bowling leagues?
Did we just miss the mistletoe? Did all the clues elude us?
Does she believe in Santa Claus or just Santa Gertrudis?
And if we looked would we see sign of reindeer in the pen
Or would we just convince ourselves the goat got out again?
And after we'd all gone to bed would they join in a hymn
And sing that little manger song they learned in Bethlehem?
I guess that it don't matter much if cows believe or not.
We'll fork her out a flake of hay and head back in a trot
To celebrate our Christmas Day and all   that we espouse
And when we say our dinner grace
  we'll thank him for the cows.
For the livelihood they give us
  and life we get to share.
But do the cows have
      Christmas cheer?
  Who knows, but just beware
  If you see chicken tracks
    among the straw
  and drying chips
 You better check
 suspicious cows
  for egg nog
  on their lips.

178

TWELVE DAYS OF CHRISTMAS

On the first day of Christmas my new love gave to me a cowdog who played the trombone. (Which was okay because I knew she loved animals and she was going to veterinary school to reduce their suffering and make her contribution for the benefit of mankind. Besides, she had the best little parakeets in town.)

On the second day of Christmas my new love gave to me two circling perch. (They were in a 12 foot stock tank and were victims of a boating accident which explained why they always swam in a circle. I'd never seen a fish swim with a limp before.)

On the third day of Christmas my new love gave to me three flat mice. (She said they'd been caught in the copy machine at the alternative medicine laboratory and were suffering from toner toxicity. They'd been collated as well. Anyway, they were easy to store. I just stacked them in the spoon drawer and occasionally used one as a bookmark. I was reading <u>Of Mice and Men</u>.)

On the fourth day of Christmas my new love gave to me four troubled cats. (She said these cats had been presented to the vet school with behavioral problems. They stayed out all night, knocked over trash cans and smoked fish. You could smell the herring on their breath. She had a pickup load of sand dumped in my foyer.)

On the fifth day of Christmas my new love gave to me five pigs that sing. (I have to admit they were a bit much. I mean, where do you put a pig? I live in an apartment.)

On the sixth day of Christmas my new love gave to me six geese a goosing. (It's not like the honking wasn't bad enough but every time I'd turn around one of them was sneaking up behind me and poking me with their beak.)

On the seventh day of Christmas my new love gave to me seven sheep a sleeping. (They'd been diagnosed with narcolepsy. Well behaved, but they'd lumber around the apartment all hours of the night bumping into things and leaving little seeds everywhere. Sheep have seeds, ya know. You find them scattered on the ground everywhere sheep are.)

On the eighth day of Christmas my new love gave to me a night to remember. (Which convinced me that the nine llamas leaping and the ten hamsters coughing were worth it.)

On the eleventh day of Christmas my new love gave to me eleven Holsteins milking. (Which brought our relationship back into focus. My gosh, they were giving 70 pounds a day - each! That's a hundred gallons a day. And talk about messing on the carpet. Meals on Wheels brought two tons of hay a week and enough corn to make Jack Daniels jealous.)

On the twelveth day of Christmas I'd had enough! (She decided to specialize in marine biology with an emphasis in walrus medicine. Twelve walrus in my waterbed.... some things were not meant to be.)

I've been gone for two weeks and last I heard she was engaged to an endangered species and living in a tree.

I wish her the best.

JOE AND MARIA

THE FIRST CHRISTMAS . . . COWBOY STYLE

Now, I 'spect most of you cowboys have heard the story 'bout Christmas. How it came to be an' all, but I wanna 'splain it so y'all kin understand.

It started with this cowboy named Joe. He'd married a girl name Maria. Times was hard in them days. They's down to the crumbly jerky and one ol' paint gelding named Duke. To top it off, Maria was in the family way.

They'd been ridin' several days, with Joe mostly walkin'. They camped on the trail and Maria was gettin' tired an' ornery. Late one night, December 24th, I think, they spotted the lights of a little burg. It was a welcome sight 'cause the weather'd turned coolish.

There was only one hotel in town and Joe offered to chop wood or wash dishes for a room, but they were full up. The clerk said they could lay out their rolls in the livery stable. Git'em outta the wind anyway.

So Joe built 'em a nest in one of the stalls and went out to rustle up some grub. When he came back, Maria was fixin' to have that baby. Well, Joe panicked.

He laid out his slicker, fluffed up the straw and ran down the street lookin' for a doc. By the time he got back Marie'd done had the baby. It was a boy. She had him wiped off an' wrapped up in Joe's extra longjohn shirt.

Joe was proud and Maria was already talkin' baby talk to the little one. They discussed what to call him. Joe wouldn't have minded if they'd named him Joe, Jr. but Maria wanted to call him Jesus. A promise she'd made before Joe knew her.

Maria was tuckered. Jesus was sleepin' like a baby and Joe was tickin' like a two dollar watch. Fatherhood had hit him like a bag of loose salt! Just then he heard singin'.

In through the door of the livery come six Mexican sheepherders. They gathered around the baby and said he sure looked good. "Niño especial," they said. Then they laid out some tortillas and commenced to visit.

Suddenly three fellas rode right into the livery. There was two Indian braves and a black cavalry scout. They told Joe that they'd had a vision and followed a star right to this very spot.

Joe said, "No kiddin'?"

"Shore nuf," they said. This was a special baby. He'd be a chief someday. This was good news to Joe. Not only that, they'd brought three buffalo hides, two handmade blankets and a little poke of gold dust which they gave to Joe to use for the baby.

Joe and Maria were overwhelmed. One of the herders tied together a little crib. He packed the bottom with straw and laid a sheepskin over it. Maria laid Baby Jesus in it, and He never woke up; just gurgled and smiled.

Then the whole bunch of 'em stayed up all night talkin' 'bout Christmas.

Joe never forgot. He did his best to raise his son right and when Jesus went on to bigger and better things, Joe'd remember that night. When a handful of strangers helped his little family through a hard time. He told Jesus 'bout it when He was old enough to understand. How just a little kindness to yer fellow man can go a long way. Jesus took it to heart.

DAVE HOLL

HOW DO YOU KNOW IT'S CHRISTMAS?

So, how do you know it's Christmas?

'Cause the sheep can always tell.
      They follow a little tradition and have for quite a spell.
On Christmas Eve around midnight, the sheep, wherever they are
      All rise in quiet unison and fixate on a star.
And from their stirring comes a sound, a chuckling tra, la, la
      That weaves and builds itself into a soft melodious baaa
Which carries like a dove's lament when nights are very still
      As if they're calling for someone beyond a yonder hill.

The legend herders passed on down attributes this tradition
      To one late night in Bethlehem. A heavenly petition
Wherein a host of angels came and lured them with a song.
      The herders left in haste, they say, and stayed gone all night long.

Well, sheep don't do too well alone. They've never comprehended
      that on that night they waited up, the world was upended.

So, now when daylight shortens up and nights get long and cold
      I make my check at midnight like we've done since days of old
And if I find the flock intent and standing all around
      I listen for the heavenly host above their throaty sound
And scan the dim horizon in an effort to discern
      The sign the sheep are seeking, that their shepherds will return.

And I am but a watchman in this drama that replays
      Around the earth this time of year, and so I stand and gaze
And though I see no special star or hear no sweet noel,
      I know it must be Christmas, 'cause the sheep can always tell.

THE LAST BURRO

He was the last burro left in the dusty corral.

His two companions had been sold by the man. They were younger, stronger and finer looking even by burro standards, which are quite high. They were worth more and brought more money which was what the man needed.

Pickin's were slim. Every evening the man would stake the last burro out down below the spring to graze. During the day he went with the man and packed mud or water or rocks or wood.

One morning the man fed him a small bowl of grain. This continued for several days until the morning the man brushed him down, bobbed his tail and trimmed his long whiskers. Next thing he knew, the burro was blanketed and fit with a pack saddle. Two panyards were hung over the frame and a thick pad was laid between the forks.

The burro watched with his wise burro eyes as the man led the woman out to the hitch rail and gently lifted her up on his pack saddle. The man shouldered his own pack, picked up his walkin' stick and clucked to the burro.

The burro was old but he carried the load as easily as an old man milks a goat. From memory... automatic. As he walked down the road he passed his two younger, stronger companions. They were hitched to a water wheel and strained in their harness as they walked round and round. 'Better this than that', thought the last burro.

They walked all day. It was the cool season, his hooves were hard as iron. The woman balanced well.

The second day the woman got off and walked a while. The man tied his pack on the saddle and they walked on. As the days went by the woman got off more often and they'd stop to rest for a while.

They arrived in a town late one night. The man went in a house. The woman waited. Momentarily the man returned and led the burro around back to the stable. The burro was glad to get the saddle off. He was watered, tied in a far corner and fed some grass hay.

The burro watched as the man put a blanket in one of the stalls and laid the woman down. Time passed. Later in the night the woman walked out carrying a man-child and laid him in a hay manger.

The burro slept, as old men do, with one ear cocked. He saw the sheepmen come, he heard the singing. He'd heard it before. The burro had worked the sheep camps.

Next morning the man fed and watered the burro and left. While he was gone the woman picked up the man-child and brought him to the burro. She raised one of his tiny hands and stroked the burro's soft nose. She, herself, patted the burro's neck.

On the trip back home the woman and man-child rode on the burro's back.

As the years went by the woman would bring the growing man-child out to the corral and hold him up or set him on the burro's back. She would talk man-talk to the child. And when the burro got too old to work the man-child would come and stroke his nose and give him a handful of grain.

One day the burro could no longer get up. He became frightened. The woman and the grown young man came to the corral and held his head in their laps. They patted his rough coat and stroked his soft nose. Eventually the burro closed his eyes. He felt a teardrop on his face. It was the last thing he ever felt.

THE DEMON CHILI

In the Hall of Fame of ranch cooks there's a name you'll never hear.
    We had him at the Bar V for a while.
In truth, I guess, he could have made the Ten Most Wanted list
    'Cause poisonin' cowboys really was his style.

I remember one October, we were at the Tanner camp.
    He cooked a pot of chili . . . Make ya sweat!
It was really pretty tasty but then later on that night
    We sounded like a bullfrog base quartet.

That next mornin' somethin' happened that had put him in a funk.
    I think he thought we'd eaten his sardines.
We were hopin' for some biscuits, maybe even sourdough
    But he heated up that mess of chili beans.

It was just a little thicker and by lunch that afternoon
    It had a crust just like a cherry pie,
Only crunchier and gritty, like an asphalt shingle is.
    We ate it, but it made young Miltie cry.

And for supper he served chili. "That's all you get," he said
    Then wiped a tar-like substance from his beard.
An image of La Brea came to mind as I dug in,
    My spoon broke off and slowly disappeared.

But that evenin' in the bunkhouse it was like a battlefield.
    Blankets billowed with each unexpected round,
Huge explosions, whistling tracers, not to mention S.B.D.'s
    But nowhere was a gas mask to be found.

Breakfast came. We had more chili. He reheated it again.
    It concentrated down like toxic waste.
Our ol' bellies were rebelling as he chipped us out a chunk.
    It left a sort of diesel aftertaste.

Gus had found a box of ear tags, so that's what we had for lunch.
    But supper brought no edible release
'Cause he served a chili cinder block. It was standing on all fours.
    He hack-sawed off each one of us a piece.

So that night in desperation we convened to make a plan,
      Shoot the cook - drag his entrails through the fire.
But we realized that wouldn't work, the chili would live on,
      Complete destruction was what we'd require.

That next mornin' found us gathered at the east side cookhouse door
      With pitchforks, shotguns, bayonets and spears.
Bob had found a propane burner and a couple carbide guns,
      We charged the kitchen like the grenadiers.

Total chaos! Immolation! Not a pan or plate survived!
      The walls caved in, the trusses all were bared!
But still standing in the ruins like Godzilla with the gout,
      The chili demon growled at us and glared.

"I can't take it!" cried ol' Jimbo, his machete o'er his head,
      He hacked it into little greasy specks.
The cook watched the execution, then Jim turned to him and said,
      "You fix us somethin' good, or Bud, yer next!"

We had two more days of cow work and we ate like we were kings
      But that cook's concoction still gives me the shakes.
It's come back to haunt me daily, been recycled don't you see...
      I smell chili every time I hit the brakes.

THE VEGETABLE DEFAMATION TRIAL

It was a severe case of vegetable defamation
the makin's of a landmark case of harassment and abuse.
The plaintiff, a Miss Parsley was demanding compensation
of one Paul Pierre Potato and, to-be-specified produce.

"So how do you plead, Mr. Tater?"
  "Not guilty but let me relate
    I'm a victim of mass inflammation,
      au gratined and smeared on a plate,
        laid next to a lecherous cutlet
      whose gravy kept touching my cheese.
    It was all I could do to keep silent.
  Then I felt the promiscuous peas.

Nudging their firm little bodies,
  assuming themselves in my space,
    It was clear they had eyes for the cutlet
      and longed for his gravy embrace.
        And there I lay lumpy and fighting my pain,
      ignored as the fork stirred their lust.
    The shame that I felt in their amorous twine
  sorely tempted, but cry out I must,

'Decorum', I prompted, 'Remember you're food!
  Presentation is half of the meal!
    Take pride in your placement and dress up your ranks,
      we're the chef's culinary ideal.
        A painting in fiber, a sculpture in glaze,
      a feast for a gourmet's eye view!
    You're acting like leftovers, reheated lumps.
  The diners will think that we're stew.'

Alas, twas no use, they continued to mix
  till we looked like a discarded cud.
    Bereft of all pride, depraved by the scene,
      I peered up out of the mud.
        And there on the edge, immune to the drama
      in which I was hopelessly scrounged,
    A vision of verdant vegetaciousness . . .
  Miss Parsley, provocative, lounged."

"At last," said the judge, "you have got to the point."
    "Your honor, I meant no offense.
        My ardor, my shame, my hope gave me voice
        and I lost all track of good sense.
            I lay in the wallow of half eaten peas,
        a gristle and gravy abyss,
    So I asked, 'Why's a cute little sprig like yourself
ensconced on a platter like this?' "

"Is that all?" asked the judge, "That was intentional."
    Potato replied in retort, "The plate was slick,
        I started congealing, I grabbed at her frond for support.
        I got cheese on her ramus. She drew back aghast,
    'Don't think I've not heard of your couch!
    You dirty old tuber, when I'm through with you,
you'll wish you were powdered, I'll vouch.'

It only got worse. Said I looked like a chip.
    Some fast food turned up by a plow.
    'A chip!' I decried. 'A step below fried!'
    She said, 'I'm referring to cow!'
        It was all I could take, 'You incipient fern,
    you nourishment of last resort!
    It's no wonder nobody eats parsley.'
She said, 'Greaseball, I'll see you in court.'"

Vegetable harassment was the charge the judge adjudicated on.
    The retribution swift and a sentence some might think unduly rash
for Potato was convicted and was corned beef hash by dawn
    and Miss Parsley was, as usual, just scraped into the trash.

THE BUMBLING ECOTERRORIST

Outside an upscale shopping mall appeared a scruffy knave.
   His hope, enlightened urbanites to please.
      He steered his stealthy mountain bike around the parking lot
and drove a stake through all the S.U.V's.

Plus two Volkswagon buses - which incensed The Green Peace crowd
   But raised a flag and gave our man away.
      His handiwork was recognized by friend and foe alike,
'Twas... the bumbling ecoterrorist named Ray.

He meant well liberal pundits said but still they all would cringe
   Each time they'd read about his latest spree.
      Like going to Miami to protest the football team.
His picket sign read - "Set the Dolphins Free!"

A tragic faux pas once ensued down at the city zoo
   When bumbling Ray's intentions missed the boat.
      They caught him in the big cat's cage and fined him fifty bucks
For throwing ketchup on the leopard's coat.

For reasons only he would know, in Yellowstone one day
   He bombed the Porta Potties through and through.
      The air was thick with paper bits and fog clung to the trees.
For thirty days Old Faithful's spout ran blue.

He struck a building thinking it's some scientific lab,
   An error almost anyone could make.
      Alas it was a Toys-R-Us. But Ray was not deterred,
He helped the Beanie Babies to escape.

The movie 'bout a river running through it set him off.
   "Exploiting trout," he shouted, "is corrupt!"
      He dynamited hatcheries - released a million fish.
They floated down the river belly up.

Ray planned to burn a ski resort, in protest of some sort.
   He launched himself from high atop the cline.
      On down he flew, his skis on fire, directly toward the lodge
Where stylish bums and bunnies tippled wine.

He cleared the rail out on the deck and crashed a birthday bash.
   The kids looked up and saw a human flare
      That blew their candles out then relit 'em instantly.
Then hit the life size chainsaw sculptured bear.

And on and on his exploits raged with olive oil spills
    and mutilations that gave good folks pause
        Like body piercing spotted owls, which had a bad effect
on big donations to the nature cause.

Till finally all the eco clubs dried up from lack of funds
    which left no one to go poor Raymond's bail
        And so he sat reliving all his well intentioned deeds
Until some scoundrels broke him out of jail.

Rejected by the terrorists whose image he had stained
    and greenies he'd embarrassed one by one
        He fell in with this shady bunch who let him do his thing
And went his way a proud Republican.

TROLLING FOR BUFFALO

Buffalo Bob took the call on his cellular phone. I caught the last of the conversation ". . . and if that don't work try a shot. No . . . not a tranquilizer, a 30-30. At least you'll be able to eat the meat."

"Escaped buffalo pose a problem," he said after hangin' up. "That fellow was callin' from West Virginia. I told him a trick that worked for me . . . trolling."

Bob explained that a few years back he and Dave bought twelve head of buffalo from a grain farmer on the plains of Colorado. Bought'em over the phone. *The price was right.* They arrived in the small town of Flagler and took a motel room. Three days later they were still tryin' to gather the twelve head.

The first day they built a trap out of panels in the quarter section pasture. The trap was big enough to fit the U.S.S. Eisenhower! They baited it with alfalfa and spent all afternoon tryin' to coax, drive and trick the suspicious buffalo herd into the trap. They ignored it like fat trout in a well fished stream.

That night they called a noted wildlife veterinarian who had buffalo experience. The vet arrived the next day armed with a tranquilizer gun and enough ammo to put Yellowstone Park to sleep for a fortnight.

They drove out to the herd and re-enacted the stampede from *Dances with Wolves,* but hit nary a buffalo.

Concerned with the expense of the tranquilizer, Bob and Dave built a buffalo blind outta tumbleweeds. They parked the vet with his trusty musket behind the tumbleweeds and chased buffalo by him for two hours. Unfortunately 'Dr. Dead Eye' couldn't hit the top of his head with a chafing dish. Not one bull's-eye.

The third morning found Bob and Dave making excuses to the grain farmer. "Well," he said, "do what you can, *they're yours.* I've got to go to Dad's place and haul a dead calf to the dump."

A light flickered somewhere in Buffalo Bob's desperate brain. He remembered tryin' to drag a dead buffalo calf out of a field. The herd went crazy and followed the calf through some primitive protective instinct. He actually had to get the tractor into 4th High to stay ahead and get out of the gate!

"Bring that dead calf over here. I want to try somethin'."

The farmer complied, even though it was a Hereford cross.

Bob stationed a man by the trap gate and circled the herd draggin' the dead calf behind his pickup. The buffalo cows went berserk and started chasin' the calf. Bob made a couple more circles stirrin' 'em up and on the third pass drove straight into the trap. The herd followed like greyhounds chasin' the mechanical rabbit!

"Wow!" I said, as the light dawned, "Trolling for buffalo. So that's what you advised your caller from West Virginia."

"Yeah. I don't know if it'll work, though," said Bob. "His buffalo is loose in a lady's backyard on the nice side of town."

193

WILDERNESS WALL

If you've been losing sleep at night about the public lands,
Yer not alone. We're all concerned
with changes wrought by man.
The wilderness. To have and hold is what it's all about
And we can Save the Wilderness!
By keepin' people out.
By Audubon, you know I'm right. It's humans who befoul
The habitat of prairie dog,
of elk and spotted owl.
A wall... We need a giant wall! To hold the riff raff back
But since they own the public lands,
we'll prob'ly catch some flack,
So I propose the following: A Theme Park by the Wall.
A simulated wilderness,
man-made, au natural.
The next best thing to bein' there. We'll call it **WillderWorld!**
A place where you can get moosed-out,
get badgered, skunked or squirreled!
Immerse yourself in water fowl. Commune with ancient trees,
And though they seem so real to you,
they're all facsimiles!
That's right, my friends, a Theme Park that's politically correct.
No tame coyotes or dancing bears
to lessen the effect.
At **WillderWorld** organophobes will love our guarantee,
"No living thing was sacrificed
to build this park for thee."

Imagine trees with concrete bark beneath a glassed-in dome.
Stalagmites rise from old Cheez Whiz
in caves of styrofoam.
A carbonated geyser that awaits your beck and call,
Just put a quarter in the slot
and watch the water fall!
Then travel down our Nature Trail. This ride is really neat.
See hibernating bear rugs sleep
and never leave your seat!
See bullfrogs made of fiberglass eye plastic dragonflies
And get the perfect snapshot 'cause
they never blink their eyes!
Ceramic deer and pop-up wolves in thrilling life-like scenes!
See automated leaping fish
in bubbling brook machines!
Synthetic birds that lip synch tunes and fly on hidden wires
While Bambi grazes Astro Turf
on tiny rubber tires!
And finally, as a final treat, we've one last mem'ry planned,
Our Rangers, dressed in chipmunk suits
will eat out of your hand!
The tour just takes an hour but, if you don't want to go
Just wait in the Museum Shop
and buy the video
And if you're still not satisfied, when leaving you can view
the posh resort, beyond the Wall,
we call Camp David Two!
Plus, you'll be sleepin' easier knowin' all the cash you blew
Will help protect the wilderness
from folks like me and you!

THE MOUNTAIN

Nobody rides the Mountain top when Winter's locked her jaws.
The Mountain bears the brunt alone, his shoulder to the claws.

She carves great gashes down his flank like butchers flensing sheep
And howl, you cannot know the word. She never lets him sleep.

And on his peak she wreaks her wrath. He reaches Heaven-bound
But she has placed a crown of ice and turned Hell upside down.

My parka hood is fringed with frost. It's hard to get my wind.
I stand hard on the timberline feeling freshly skinned.

The sweat is drippin' down my neck. It's twenty-two below.
I came to tell the Mountain top, "Just three more months to go.

"You're not alone," I shout to him, "There's others just like you
Who make their stand upon the Earth and see the battle through

The daily grind to just get by against all Earthly odds
And keep the faith though they might feel forsaken by the gods."

My words are snatched up by the wind and shatter in the air.
The Winter scatters spoken broken pieces everywhere.

I strain to see the highest ridge that climbs the steep terrain
That's whipped until its frothy edge is like a horse's mane

Then disappears into the storm, the maelstrom, the shriek,
That smothers and obliterates the nearly hidden peak.

The Winter bellows out her rage. She's comin' down the face.
I turn downhill and cower in the timber's tall embrace.

Her blizzard fingers flow around the trees and follow me.
I stop and squint back toward the top but white-out's all I see.

I meant to bring some small relief. I wanted just to say
No man or mountain stands alone. We're all the Maker's clay.

"But I can only cringe and squeak," I whisper up the slope
But then the Mountain answered back, "Go, friend. You left me hope."

TROUTING

Not quite twilight.

The tip of my rod silhouettes against a bright patch of water.

It dips in rhythm with the current . . . or is it with the beat of my heart?

Somewhere beneath the glassy reflection and tumbling whitewater swims a trout.

I reel in a few feet of line thinking he will notice. Of course, he notices. He watched me ease into the water from the bank. He is watching my shadow. He saw my bait hit the surface. He has been aware of my presence since I forged the river a hundred yards upstream. I have walked into his home without wiping my feet. I am standing on his kitchen floor. I am dragging bait back and forth across his table.

Wouldn't you notice if a stranger walked into your den, turned off your TV and started throwing M & M's in your lap? Certainly, you would.

But the trout is innocent. He has no way to comprehend my devious intent. He does not understand premeditation, temptation, selling your soul, giving your all, monofilament line, tartar sauce, the Bernouli force, or fish and chips.

I bob and tickle the line, enticing him. I imagine him nonchalantly beating his tail, occasionally adjusting his ailerons, holding himself steady in the sweeping current, conspicuously ignoring my bait which is now performing quirky gyrations inches from his face.

Does he relate to the mama killdeer who fakes a broken wing to draw predators away from her nest? Does he know that lions look for crippled gnus? Does he know panhandlers attack those who amble and gander? Surely I must think so, else why have I adopted the mind set of a dysfunctional earthworm.

I feel the thump of a nibble. Or is it the weights banging on the smooth stones? It thumps three times then quits. Impatient, I reel in. Part of the bait is gone. I reworm with the nagging thought that it's just a little fish or even a sucker.

Back in the water . . . in the sweet spot. The worm looks good enough to eat. I am convinced that I know what tastes good to a fish.

I wait. He must be sniffing this tempting truffle. So round, so firm, so wiggly, dancing in front of his face, the aroma surrounding him, flowing over his slick scales, filling his nostrils, his gills, his fish bowl with baking bread, barbecuing steaks, mint chocolate chips, new mown hay, smoked ham and peanut butter peach cobbler étouffée with raspberry sauce and jalapeños!

I sense the moment, the impending strike, the expectation holds me still to the point of breathless.

The tip of my rod dips in rhythm with the current . . . or is it with the beat of my heart? It doesn't matter, they are the same.

SPRINGTIME IN THE ROCKIES

When it's springtime in the Rockies and my lips are turning blue
I'll be slogging through the blizzard like a brain dead caribou....

Ah, springtime.
That first hint of life beginning anew, the annual transformation,
    the earth taking off its long johns, shedding its skin,
clearing its throat in long tubercular coughs that turn rain into
birdshot,
    sleet into ice, ice into snowflakes shaped like goatheads or bob wire,
not falling but slicing by you like shrapnel, sandblasting your face,
    freezing your rein hand into a claw and turning forty-five degrees and
balmy into assault with intent to stupefy.

Ah, springtime.
Brave wild flowers bursting from winter's blanket,
    the trill of the mountain bluebird, the exultation of a rushing brook,
the whine of a spinning tire, the splock of pliers dropped from your
hand,
    the rattle of mudtags on a feedlot steer that makes him sound
when he walks like a limping Moroccan bride.
    That half brave, half scared elation of aiming your truck toward the
muddy dirt road ruts like a boat captain docking with the current,
    like Fast Eddy runnin' one down the rail.

Ah, springtime.
The anticipation of a new bride or a butterfly waking in his cocoon.
    Like Christmas Eve with all the presents of summer waiting
to be opened. The weatherman declaring winter's over,
    angels celebrating the vernal equinox by hosing out Gabriel's
hog confinement shed, drip drying their laundry between
    the mountain tops and revving up the windchill machine
for one last recalibration.

Ah, springtime,
Best viewed through a picture window settin' by the fire.

Once again you'll hear me promise, you'll be hearing from me soon.
When it's springtime in the Rockies, I'll be calling from Cancun...

MISERABLE

March came in like a lion and left the door open
　　It's blowed like a banshee for weeks
I saddle and ride like some kind of robot
　　She builds up a temper and shrieks

The constant thrumming that grates on my skin
　　And pulls on my collar and coat
Like a CPR leech that's hooked to my lungs
　　And suckin' the breath from my throat

I squint through the haze for a sign of the bunch
　　I'm s'posed to be checkin' the stock
But great herds of sagebrush stampede through the dust
　　And often a cow is a rock

My patience wears thin and my horse bears the brunt
　　Of frustrations rubbin' me raw
I've ground my pore teeth 'til they've taken an edge
　　My rein hand is stiff as a claw

And there ain't no relief in the bunkhouse at night
　　It howls and the demons rave on
It whistles and moans through the cracks in the wall
　　'Til all hope of sleepin' is gone

My ears ache like crazy. My hair even hurts
　　The drumming plays on in my head
It pounds until mornin'. It takes all my strength
　　To get up and git outta bed

I'm dry as a mummy and I plan to get up though
　　It's easy to rationalize
But the horses need fed and led to the creek
　　So I clean the dirt from my eyes

And walk to the door. I hear the wind knockin'
　　I'm filled with a big dose of dread
I sag in my boot tops, it's miserable out
　　Ya know, I could braid rawhide instead

The boss ain't comin' for a couple more days, but
　　The code says a cowboy should ride
Come hell or high water, but I think today
　　I'll just be miserable . . . inside

THE OUTFITTER'S JERKY

In hunting camp an outfitter leaned down and stirred the fire.
His client belched contentedly and said, "Might I inquire,
That jerky you been chewin' on... could I just try a bit?
I fancy I'm a connoisseur with tongue and palate fit
To ferret out the kind of beast, perhaps the cut of meat
From whence you sliced the bloody strap and held it to the heat."
The packer passed a little piece to test the boastful claim,
The hunter sniffed the charred remains, bit in and then proclaimed,

"I taste a hint of kidney fat. The tang of creosote.
A wistful note of pine tree sap lays pungent in my throat.
What's this? A waft of ungulate, the glue of hoof and horn,
An Eohippus redolence, the musk of unicorn.
Peculiar, though I must admit, I can't tell heads nor tails.
I'm left with just the essence of burnt hair and roofing nails.
I pride myself on this small skill but if you could be swayed,
Pray, tell me from what animal is this here jerky made?"

The packer picked his grimy teeth, his filthy knife, the tool.
"It all began," he spit and said, "with one ol' stubborn mule
Named Demon, and the name sure fit. Worst mule I've ever seen.
Last hunt when we were comin' out he really got down mean.
It took us nearly half a day to git the sucker packed.
He'd buck the panyards off each time and roll clear on his back.
He kicked and struck and strained the knots,
        he bit and brayed and gassed,
We finally had to tie him down to get the elk made fast.

At last he stood and glared at us, resigned but not unbowed.
We started down the mountain side as best the load allowed.
We had to cross a narrow trail above a closed down mine.
The Demon went to pullin' back, I'd hitched him last in line.
He balked, then had a mental lapse... forgot that he was tied!
And then just like a fumbled punt he cartwheeled down the side.
I quit my horse and bared my knife, and dove between the mules.
I slashed the halter shank between the mule train and the fools.

Down we went, an avalanche of elk and mule and man,
The antlers racked the Coleman stove, I kissed the frying pan.
The propane tank was hissin', the elk meat held on tight,
I hit the shale below the mine, the mule dropped outta sight.
Above my head a blinding flash exploded in my eyes.
And when the dust had settled, the mule had vaporized.
I peeked down in the mine shaft through the timbers and the smoke
And saw ol' Demon at long last had shed his final yoke.

He never knew what hit him, so at least it wasn't cruel."

"Gosh," the hunter shook his head, "I'm sorry 'bout yer mule. But back to this here jerky, do you share your recipes?"

"Well, wuddn't nuthin' to it. I just picked it off the trees."

RHINO LOVE

Dr. Fosse, once of Pretoria, commented that most of my stories involved wrecks. I said I think it's the nature of business. Matter of fact, I said, you could haul a bunch of cowboys from the U.S. to South Africa, turn 'em loose on the Savannah and they'd be in a wreck as quick as one of 'em broke out his lasso.

"Actually," he said, "We're quite capable of creating our own." Then he told me about Martha and Arthur, two star crossed rare white rhinos.

In a governmental gesture of goodwill, South Africa agreed to ship Arthur to Tanzania to mate with Martha. Brilliant veterinarians, competent game management officials, long winded reproductive specialists and the press discussed at length the procedures involved and the benefits that would accrue with these international relations.

They soon discovered that rhinos cycle according to the length of daylight hours. Martha, on Equatorial Daylight Time, was never quite synchronized with Arthur, on Tropic of Capricornical Time. When he was randy she had a headache and when she was cuddly he was not in the mood.

However our team of deep thinkers figgered a way around it. They'd artificially inseminate Martha! I can just see these characters squatting under an Acacia tree, breakin' out a case of Congo Lite and drawing their plans in the dirt with pipettes.

But since Martha wasn't cooperating anyway and no sweet smelling rhino geldings were around, they decided to collect Arthur's semen with an electro ejaculator.

Enlisting the aid of their agricultural engineers, they built a homemade ejaculator out of wire, copper electrodes, a hand crank and lots of electrical tape.

Arthur was quite tame so on the big day they led him out with a loop around the horn and tied him to a thorn tree. With proper lubrication, the head mogul inserted the prod and set the cowboys to crankin'. Alas, Arthur showed no response.

"He's probably packed with dry feces which is interfering with conduction of the current," interjected the rhino physiologist.

So they attempted to clean him out while he stood there compliantly. Then they tried again... no luck.

"Being a desert beast, possibly there is a lack of internal moisture," observed the rhino hydrologist. "How 'bout an enema?"

They hung a twenty gallon container from the tree, inserted a hose and the water disappeared like a Diet Sprite in the Sahara. "More water!" they cried. Another twenty gallons were fetched and inserted. Arthur stood unruffled.

Agreeing that should have certainly lubricated Arthur, the chief acting assistant veterinary cowboy technician strode forth and inserted his plastic sleeved arm to evacuate the bowel. Arthur had had enough.

He clamped his powerful aft torpedo door shut just above the hapless white smocked invader's elbow. They thundered off through the brush! The crew followed in the Land Rover, eating their sack lunches and videoing the chase.

A hundred yards down the track the offending appendage popped out followed by 40 gallons of pent up colored water. The invader lay like a drowned muskrat left in the furrow. Arthur raced off to the other side of the game park.

"Yer right," I told Dr. Fosse, "we couldn't have done it better."

GODDESS OF THE HUNT

Diana, goddess of the hunt, stands as a Roman heroine to a long line of female hunters. Even today there are many who have followed in her spoor that deserve to have their name written in mythology.

Our Diana, we'll call her Center-Fire Charlotte, is well known for her prowess up and down Hyde Creek in the high and wild country of central Idaho. The legend goes that one morning Charlotte was on her way to work in town when she spotted a bunch of does grazing by the reservoir. She climbed out of her car, quietly closed the door, lifted her rifle from the trunk and started after them. Sage, bunch grass, rocks, brush and pine seedlings gave way as she stalked across the clearing in her cashmere sweater, skirt and medium heels.

Single-mindedly she tracked, eye on the ridge of the dam, swatting the occasional biting fly. Cresting the ridge in a crouch she saw the deer beneath her. In the midst of the does a good sized buck reared his majestic head. Center-Fire drew down and dropped him.

She stood over the clean kill and asked the deer's forgiveness. She carefully looked all around. Sensing the all clear she decided to gut him on the spot.

Several hundred yards away, parked at the airport sat a vehicle. The local game warden was sipping coffee from a paper cup in the front seat. He heard the shot. Scanning the slope below the reservoir he spotted a suspicious movement.

A woman wielding a large knife stood above a deer. She wore only a bra. Her skirt was tucked up around the waist band of her panty hose like a Sumo wrestler's loin cloth. Cranking his binocs to 9x power, he recognized the sweating forehead of Charlotte.

By the time she had driven home, come back with the four-wheel drive, retrieved the fallen deer, cleaned up and come to work, every human in the small mountain town was aware of her Amazon exploits. Diana, goddess of the hunt had returned!

It was only fitting that on her next birthday one of the presents she would receive anonymously was a new brassiere... in hunter's fluorescent orange. Beneath each cup was sewn a strip of gunbelt complete with 30.06 shells lodged in place. Bandolaras on a cantaloupe.

No recent sightings have been made of Center-Fire Charlotte *'in uniform'*. But it is thought that she applied for a permit to conceal her weapon and now stalks the back country disguised as a Sierra Club consultant.

THE HUNTER'S SON

This is the poem of the hunter's son as he tracks the woods alone
And the beaver's revenge when he seeks to avenge
the hunter's gauntlet thrown
By choosing to pair with a grizzly bear, big, nasty and fully grown.

He was raised in the woods and meadow where ice and forest collide
In the Peace River reach where fathers still teach
their sons how to hunt and provide.
Young Scott was in search of the beaver.
The country was thick with'em then.
Traps were his love but he wasn't above a rifle shot now and again.

He snuck through the woods like a shadow
and stopped just short of a spring.
There on the bank like a person of rank sat Oscar, the Beaver King.
He was big as a Yellowknife huskie and hummin' a Rachmaninov,
Scott froze in his track, Oscar never looked back
till he heard the safety click off.

Then he rolled like a log to the water. The bullet sang just by his ear!
Though caught unaware he escaped by a hair
and Scott saw the King disappear.
Scott cursed his bad luck 'cause ol' Oscar had beaten him just like before
So he turned on the trail, like a dog tuckin' tail
and headed back home sad and sore.

But his path was impeded in progress by a bear with a griz pedigree.
He was hungry and large, so when he made a charge
Scott climbed up a poplar tree.
He clum till the tree started bendin', twenty feet up off the ground
He sat in a crotch while the bear carved a notch
each time that he circled around.

He climbed within inches of Scotty and scared the bee jee outta him,
He snorted and growled and about disemboweled
the poplar tree, root to limb.
But he finally backed off, reconsidered, like only a grizzly bear could,
He shook a big paw and bid au revoir, then disappeared into the wood.

Though shaken, Scott felt he had triumphed,
there from his perch in the bleachers.
The vast human brain will always remain the master of God's lesser creatures.
But the sight he beheld left him chastened, outwitted by over-achievers.
The bear reappeared, new help commandeered,
with Oscar, the King of the Beavers.

THE THERAPEUTIC GOAT

Goat: 1) The most widely domesticated ruminant in the world
          2) Cantankerous person, as in "Old Goat"
          3) Ancient canon thought to ward off equine disease

Blaine was in Saskatchewan adding to his revolving horse collection, when the seller suggested he take a goat along as well. "Ya know, they have a calming effect on horses. As well as disease prevention."

"Where might I get one?" inquired Blaine. "I have one right here for only $25," replied the seller, injecting ol' Billy into the innocent Blaine. Goat and horse climbed into the trailer.

On the trip home to Pincher Creek Blaine became aware of Billy's strong, some would say unpleasant, odor. It only disappeared when he got above 60 km/h.

Billy became king of the barnyard. He spent time with his original equine companion but generously made himself available to the other horses as well as occasional bulls that required goat therapy.

Blaine was pleased with the harmony that Billy lent to the homestead. And, if the smell bothered Blaine, he never said. It is entirely possible that Blaine was olfactorily impaired due to his constant exposure to the purulent, putrifying parasitic infestations and assorted unsavory, malodorous pestilence that occurred in his daily practice of veterinary medicine.

However, it became a constant source of inquiry by farmers bringing stock by the clinic, as in, "O-o-o-o-e-e-e! Vat's dat smell, eh?"

"It's a goat," explained Blaine, "It's been said they have curative powers." "Yer ta vet," they'd say, "You don't belief dat do you?" You could hear the fear in their voices as they imagined Blaine sending stinking ol' Billy home with them as companion for their trembling llama.

Soon, female goats were added to the menagerie as company for Billy. Goats begat goats begat more goats. They ate everything in sight. When they reached their peak population, the mob numbered 27. They would swarm a full grown conifer or decorative hedge like locusts and strip it bare. Finally under threat of banishment from the house, Blaine got rid of all the goats except Billy, who continued to reign supreme from his throne atop a round bale feeder in the colt corral.

One afternoon a buyer came by to look at some colts. Blaine led him into the corral. Billy was ensconced on his perch, head peaking through the tubular steel frame.

"Whoeee! What in the blasphemous, offensive, scatological, politically incorrect bodily function is that!" the buyer asked, covering his burning eyes and holding his nose. "It's a goat," said Blaine. "It smells dead," choked the buyer.

Blaine gave a second look. Billy was sitting where he always sat, right on top of the round bale feeder. Except his head was at an odd angle where it poked under the steel. Upon closer examination there were other indicators of an accidental barnyard suicide of several days duration, like a balloonish appearance and slippin' of the hair. "Yer right," said Blaine pausing, "I thought that bale was lastin' longer than usual."

GOOSE SEASON

Goose season is on us again. When the great majestic Canadian honkers course through the pale winter skies like waves of bombers rolling toward Germany in World War II.

The goose population is on the rise. Even to the point that some city dwellers are complaining of goose ditritus and effluvia (sounds like names for mythical Greek hillbillies) despoiling city parks, jogging paths and sidewalks.

To wheat farmers on the flyway, the problem is less one of sanitation and more one of production. They eat the newly sprouted wheat.

Keith farms in north central Oklahoma. Geese have been regular squatters in his wheat fields for years but the goose population explosion is taking its toll on his crop and his patience.

Last season some of his city friends asked to hunt pheasant on his place. They were welcome, of course. Keith took them to the backside of his farm where he'd left some cover and dropped them off. When he picked them up later in the afternoon he drove by his wheat fields. New growth was peekin' up and adding unnatural green patches to the brown winter landscape. He also noted five hundred geese had flown in and set up camp. They were busily plucking the sprouts.

"Boys," he said to his three Boone & Crockett buddies, "climb in the back and I'll take you for a goose run."

They did. Keith got on the inside of the hot wire, put it in 4-wheel drive and started down the edge of the field. The hunters were crowded in the bed of the pickup. Keith was doin' 35 mph when he got broadside of the geese. He wheeled hard to port, stomped the gas and closed the distance in a matter of seconds.

He was doing fifty miles an hour when he flew through the flurry of geese! The sky was black with them. The raucous honking was deafening. Mud was banging in the wheel wells but he heard nary a shot.

In the blink of an eye he was clear of the geese, although it was impossible to see out the windshield. Apparently, in an effort to lighten their load, they had performed a cloacal evacuation as they sailed over the cab.

A glance at his intrepid hunters soon led him to realize why their guns were silent. They looked like they had been in an oatmeal storm. Maybe a Cream of Wheat drive-by creaming, or had stepped on a butterscotch mine.

Goose droppings splattered their Eddie Bauers, smeared their Land's End, coated their Cabela's, lambasted their L.L. Beans, splattered, smeared, blinded, bluffed and buffeted them as the blizzard of geese had flown over at ground zero.

Their spokesman removed his Smith and Wesson sunglasses, revealing the only bare skin on his face. He looked like a pallid raccoon.

"They shot first," he said, "We didn't have a chance!"

VETERINARY DIAGNOSTIC VOICE MAIL

Hello. You have reached the automated voice mail of **Triple A, Aardvarks Are Us, All Creatures Great and Small Veterinary Clinic, Animal Health Supply, Grooming, Boarding and Training, and Counseling Center.** *If you have a credit card limit of no less than five thousand dollars please press one, if not please hold.*

[1] Thank you. If your problem concerns a pet - including dogs, cats, small rodents, reptiles, cockatiels, highway accidents and other creatures where cost is no object. . . please press one.
If you have livestock who's value is dependent on a fickle, unpredictable, often cruel market BUT you have a good job in town, a wife with a job, federal disaster insurance or land and farm equipment that can be used as collateral. . . please press two.

[2] If you have a poultry problem. . .press one for the Campbells Soup buyer. If you are a pork producer. . .press two for counseling and hysteria prevention. If your problem concerns cattle. . .press three.

[3] If the condition is serious enough (over $500) and you can bring the animal to the clinic. . . press one.
If the condition is not life threatening or you do not have a stock trailer. . . press two.

[2] If you have already been treating this animal yourself for weeks. . . press one.

[1] If the animal is ambulatory. . . press 1
If the animal is recumbent. . . . press 2
If the animal is comatose. . . . . .press 3

[2] If the animal has been down for less than two days. . .press one.

[1] If the animal is still eating and drinking. . .press one.
If the animal is not eating but still has a detectable pulse. . . press two.

[2] We have now reached the critical stage in this automated voice mail Diagnostic Situation Prognosis Assessment Device. Your prognosis is: Poor to partly cloudy - estimated cost $112.00. Add $5 for weekend and after hours - satisfaction barometer minus 3
If you would like to have the veterinarian make a house call. . .press one
If you want to kiss it off and bite the bullet press two for Johansen's Hide and Tallow.

[2] Have a nice day.

THE C-SECTION

The phone rang. It was four o'clock. . . the other four o'clock.
  A worried voice came on the line, "Sorry to wake ya, Doc,
    But I've got a calvy heifer I think's in trouble, some.
    I can't see nothin' but the tail. I'm wonderin', could ya come?"

Next thing I know I'm in his barn and starin' at this beast.
        Ten feet tall, she was, I swear, and big as a bus, at least.
    I laid a ladder 'gainst her flank. A C-section, I decide.
        After proper preparations there's a window in her side.

I poked my head inside the hole to have a look around
        A pair of parakeets flew out and fluttered to the ground,
Followed by a barkin' dog and blur of Gambel's quail.
        A hunter in fluorescent orange, hot on the covey's tail.

I climbed on in and smelled the air. No doubt, Progesterone.
        I leaned against the rumen wall and heard a slide trombone!
A corps of cuds came chomping by in step with a marching band
        All tooting on a catheter. I was Alice in Kidneyland.

        A school of pies came slicing by, meringues, mangos and minces
            And dignitaries like the Queen and Michigan Pork Princess.
        A set of Holstein heifers with their tassels all a'twirl,
            The Sheep Producer's lobbyist and Snap On calendar girl.

On they came, the A.I. techs with pipette, fife and drum,
        A pair of unborn senators, Fetaldee and Fetaldum.
This entire cast of characters was headed for the womb
        And ridin' drag in this parade was me behind a broom.

        I passed a Winchell's Donut Shop at Pancreas and Colon
            And saw a New Age singles group reliving lives and trollin'
        Then took a left on Ileum and asked the Pelvic Nerve
            Where I could find the Uterus. His Dendrite made a curve

And pointed to the Oviduct that seemed to swing and sway.
        A brightly blinking neon sign said, "BABY CALF - THIS WAY",
The cotyledons bumped my head as I went slidin' down
        "There he is," I said at last. The calf had run aground.

I hefted up a cloven hoof and started for the door.
        Then like a flash the lights came on! I slipped upon the floor,
        A scream like I ain't never heard was ringin' in my head.
            I opened up my eyes and saw me standin' by my bed.

My wife was clingin' to the post and tangled in the sheets.
  The slide trombone had died away as had the parakeets.
    I slowly came awake to find my dream had gone kaput.
    I looked down at her layin' there and let go of her foot!

MISS COMMUNICATION

The receptionist was puzzled by the answering machine.
All the message said was 'WHACKER'.
"Whacker? Wonder what that means?"

Dr. Beattie said, *"I think I know. I had a call last night*
Just before I closed the clinic but he never said outright

Exactly what his problem was. He wanted Dr. Rice.
I explained he'd left but maybe I could offer some advice.
He hemmed and hawed a minute then confided in my ear,"
"It's really kinda personal-like." *"Well, we don't treat humans here."*

"No! There's nothin' wrong with me, I'm fine. That isn't what I mean.
It's just that you're the lady vet and my story's not too clean."
"I understand, but I've been trained to do what male vets do,
Although I've never had the urge to scratch myself and chew."

"Well, it just don't seem quite proper but, I guess yer professional,
I'm a cowman out on Gun Club Road. The problem's with my bull.
I noticed it this evenin' on my way back home from town.
He was standin' by the culvert. It was draggin' on the ground."

"On the ground? Can you elaborate what you're referring to?"
"It was sorta like a python that had ate an overshoe!
It was hangin' like a lead rope! I can't say it on the phone!
I should'a called the other vet. He's got one of his own . . .

A bull, I mean! Aw, hell, er, heck! Dang it, Doc! What should I do?"
"You just bring him in tomorrow. Dr. Rice will be here, too.
I've made some notes about your case. I'll leave it on your chart
But it would help if you could just describe the injured part."

"It's an owie on his...you know, his..." he paused to gather slack,
"On his tally..." *"On his tally?"* "Oh, shoot! I'll call you back!"

The receptionist was puzzled by the answering machine...
All the message said was 'WHACKER'.

COWBOY CONFUSION

At times a cowboy's lingo can result in some confusion.
    Which brings a clash of cultures to a head.
    Mo and I were breedin' heifers, artificially, of course,
        By five we got the last one finally bred.

We headed into Vera's place for supper and a brew.
    To our surprise a crowd stood in the street.
    For tomorrow they had scheduled an Olympic Field Day
        And all the locals hankered to compete.

They'd selected the officials but they needed volunteers
    'Cause all the jobs weren't filled as they desired
    So they canvassed the assemblage seeking suitable recruits
        And cornered Mo and graciously inquired

In the women's cycling contest, would he consent to be a judge?
    Mo swallowed hard and gave his beer a quaff.
    Said he, somewhat embarrassed, "I doubt I'm qualified, besides,
        I'm sure I can't get twenty-eight days off!"

THE CALVING NIGHTY

I slept and dreamed of sunny beaches, sea shells, sand and kelp.
"I'VE GOT HER IN THE CALVING BARN. I'M GONNA NEED SOME HELP."
The waves were crashing over me, the sea gulls dived and ducked.
"SHE CALVED ALL RIGHT ALL BY HERSELF BUT JUNIOR'S NEVER SUCKED."

I woke to find my husband up and lookin' woebegone.
"IT'LL ONLY TAKE A MINUTE, YOU CAN LEAVE YOUR NIGHTY ON."
Next thing I know I'm in the barn. It smelled like creosote.
I'd pulled on his old overshoes and my ol' chorin' coat.

"IF YOU'LL DISTRACT THE COW," he said, a little bleary eyed,
"I'LL TRY AND GATHER UP THE CALF WHILE SHE'S PREOCCUPIED."
I tried to make a feeble wave. She didn't take the bait.
"YOU'VE GOT TO JUMP AROUND A BIT. JUST CLIMB UP ON THE GATE."

I stepped up on the second board and yelled with all my might.
She nearly did a somersault! I caught her eye all right.
She charged the panel where I stood, I felt the crackin' pine.
I leaped and grabbed a rafter like ol' Tarzan would the vine.

The overshoes flew off my feet, I wrapped my legs around
And hung there like a three toed sloth, my nighty hangin' down.
The cow was blowin' slobbers on my winter lingerie.
It soon became a sodden mess, exposed my exposé.

I tried to save some dignity but it was fading fast.
I felt like a piñata with a bullseye on my.... person.
Each charge she'd hook my nighty and make a bigger rip
Until I felt her cuddy breath condensing on my hip.

I'm screaming for my hubby when he finally reappeared.
The panel lay in splinters and the cow had disappeared.
"What took so long!" I shouted as I dangled overhead.
The tears were streaming down his face, he caught his breath and said,

"I DUMPED THE CALF AND BANGED MY HEAD
AND TRIED TO RACE RIGHT BACK
WHEN A MOMENTARY VISION UP AND STOPPED ME IN MY TRACK.
A NURSERY RHYME ABOUT A DISH THAT RAN AWAY WITH A SPOON
AND THERE BEFORE MY VERY EYES
THE COW JUMPED OVER THE MOON!"

It was a sorry explanation but at least I thought he tried.
I couldn't keep a straight face. We both laughed until we cried.
He still talks about my bravery and the time I used my clout
And showed'em what Victoria's secret's all about!

WHY COWBOY POETRY'S FUNNY

Cowboy poetry's mostly funny but, it's just to keep from cryin',
    'Cause the cowboy's life's a constant round of wrecks.
Every time a puncher turns around life black's him in the eye,
    Or bucks him off or bounces all his checks.

Humiliation's not enough - They get hurt, I mean a lot!
    They've perfected what it takes to set the scene
To create a situation where disaster's guaranteed,
    No matter how the angels intervene.

Think about it. If you really wanted to try and hurt yourself,
    You might call the I.R.S. up for a chat.
Or learn to juggle rattlesnakes, maybe catch'em with yer teeth,
    Or tell your wife you liked her better fat.

But the cowboy way's a sure bet. First you take a good sized beast,
    A thousand pounds and fit her with some horns
And then make her disposition like a bobcat with the piles
    And give her brains the size of grandpa's corns.

You say, Great! That sure would do it! Put that cowboy with a cow,
    Yer bound to get a wreck you won't forget.
But let's take it a step further and include another brute
    That spooks at shadows and is bigger yet,

One who jumps like Michael Jordan and dives like Moby Dick,
    Then set our cowboy up there on his back.
One more thing, we'll just connect'em with a piece of nylon rope,
    Then set back and watch our victims come untracked.

So that's why us cowboy poets write our humorous refrains,
    'Cause like I said, it's either laugh or cry.
For example, say yer horseback in the brandin' pen one day,
    And see a friend go flyin' through the sky.

We all quick go ridin' over where he's bucked off in the dirt,
    To check his pulse, if there's still one to raise.
And ... if he's livin' you start tellin' the story right away,
    And if he's dead, you wait a couple days.

KEEP IT COWBOY

Have you noticed lately how the world is changin'
That our values are adrift upon the sea.
But let me say, one man can make a difference
And I'll put it to you plain as I can be.

Can I count on you to keep it cowboy
When the bad guys have your back against the wall.
When they try and buy your soul with things that glitter
Can you shed the great temptation, after all.

Can you sort a real cowboy from a ringer
Who talks the talk but can't hold up his end
But instead of pointin' out he ain't worth shootin',
You teach him how and keep him as a friend.

For you are your brother's keeper, it is written,
And duty bound, you are, to do your part.
Will you stand up for what's right when guns are blazin'
And the weak-kneed pansies all are losing heart.

See, humans need a solid post to tie to
When the truth and what-they-want-to-hear, gets blurred.
When they can't trust all those folks they put in office
They need to know one man who keeps his word.

One whose presence in their life is a reminder
That character still matters on its own.
All I'm askin' you to do is keep it cowboy
So the world around you has a corner stone.

ABOUT THE ARTISTS.....

BOB BLACK - Nurse Johnson walked slowly into the room, a squirming bundle in her arms. She looked reluctantly into the eyes of the tired, attractive woman who occupied the white bed, "I'm sorry, Mrs. Black," she said, "it's a Bob." Bob is a primate who lives in the mesquite-rich arroyos of central Arizona with his wife and daughter, Stephanie and Samantha.

DON GILL - Wanted in several western communities for impersonating a cowboy cartoonist, Don hides out by serving as farrier, soccer coach, pick-up man and horse holder for his children. He and his wife, Denise reside in Gooding, Idaho surrounded by kids, animals and half-finished drawings.

DAVE HOLL - Dave punches cows along Aravaipa Creek in Southeastern Arizona. In his spare time he shoes horses, starts some colts and draws a few pictures. His dogs love him and his wife puts up with him.

CHARLIE MARSH - Charlie lives on the outskirts of cosmopolitan Briartown, Oklahoma with his wife Pat, Pat's mother Vade, a variety of cows, horses, dogs, cats and an outspoken bird of uncertain heritage and gender. Vagrancy and semi-unemployment have not lived up to early expectations, so he is looking now to the exploding internet market. You can look for his kitten brokering website soon. His outlook is to be traded on the NASDAQ as soon as demand begins to approach healthy supply. He still enjoys the frustrations of calf roping and will draw cartoons if the price isn't too high.

COMMENTS BY THE AUTHOR......

BAXTER BLACK - The more life changes, the more it stays the same. I'm still telling stories about God's creatures and the people who take care of them. Those farmers or cowboys or vets or horse people or any number

of combinations where an actual person makes contact with an actual cow. It's a magic place in space and time where the sparks fly, the world turns, and life rises above the mundane. It is where the action is.

There is goodness and nobility in the pursuit of tilling the soil and tending the flock. It is one of the cornerstones of humanity...feeding your fellow man, be it corn on the cob, a ribeye steak or two fish and five loaves of bread.

I'm thankful and proud to be a part, even a frivolous one, of such a grand community.

I dedicate this book to my children, Jennifer and Guy, who have given my life meaning.